THE RENEWED MIND

THE RENEWED MIND

Larry Christenson

KINGSWAY PUBLICATIONS
EASTBOURNE

© Bethany Fellowship, Inc. 1974
First British Edition 1975
Reprinted 1976
Reprinted 1977
Reprinted 1978

ISBN 0 85476 227 2

Printed in Great Britain for
Kingsway Publications Ltd
Lottbridge Drove, Eastbourne, E. Sussex BN23 6NT
by Fletcher & Son Ltd, Norwich

Preface

Do not be conformed to this world but be transformed by the renewal of your mind (Romans 12 : 1–2).

The renewed mind sees life more in terms of parables than of principles. The principles are there, of course, like an invisible foundation, supporting and undergirding. But that which the mind takes hold of, *that which makes the principle operative*, is often a picture, a story, a dramatic image. I have seen the most remarkable transformations take place in people's lives when a vivid image has been used to renew their way of thinking and acting.

The chapters of this book present a series of images and parables which have to do with Christian life and growth. It is my hope that they will offer the reader not only an understanding of biblical principles, but *practical handles* for making the principles working realities in everyday life. For the goal of a renewed mind is not simply a collection of new ideas, but a transformed life.

Pentecost 1974   LARRY CHRISTENSON

Table of Contents

PART ONE: THE RENEWED MIND DEPENDS ON GOD

BUILD THE FORMS OF HOLINESS—
LET GOD FILL THEM
EXPLORE THE MYSTERY OF GOD
DISCOVER THE SECRET OF SANCTIFICATION

CHAPTER ONE

Build the Forms of Holiness—
Let God Fill Them

Have you ever tried to break a bad habit? You set your mind to it, twist your willpower to the last turn, and think you have it just about licked—when suddenly, there it is again!

Have you ever had thoughts and ideas rise up in your mind which would make you blush with shame if they were suddenly broadcast over a loudspeaker? You don't want those thoughts. But the more you fight against them the stronger they seem to become.

Have you ever thought you were beginning to make some real progress in your Christian life, when suddenly a situation comes up which evokes hostilities in you that you didn't even know you had? You begin to wonder if your spiritual life has slipped into reverse.

Experiences like this have a common denominator. They speak of the gap which exists between what we are and what we want to be and ought to be. You might call it the holiness gap.

In Galatians 5:16, St. Paul offers some practical, down-to-earth advice about the holiness gap. It is a teaching which can lift the knapsack of drudgery from your life as a Christian, and breathe into your life a new sense of adventure, expectancy, joy—above all, a fresh anticipation of *victory*. It is a truth for those who are tired of leading defeated lives, and are ready to step over into the victory column:

"Walk by the Spirit, and do not gratify the desires of the flesh."

The Good guy and the Bad Guy—IN YOU

When we rise up in our interpreter's helicopter to view the terrain of this verse, one thing catches our eye at once. There is a battle going on! A battle between the "Spirit" and the "flesh". It is the same battle you experienced when you tried to break a bad habit, and couldn't. It's the struggle you went through when thoughts, ideas, and attitudes rose up within you that you couldn't seem to control. It's the warfare which went on within you when you felt called to a certain task, but retreated in the face of doubt and fear. In television lingo, it's the fight between the "good guy" and the "bad guy"—between the good guy and the bad guy *in you*.

Martin Luther comments on this text: "There are two contrary captains in you, the Spirit and the flesh. God hath stirred up in your body a strife and a battle: for the Spirit wrestleth against the flesh and the flesh against the Spirit. Here I require nothing else of you, but that ye follow the Spirit as your captain and guide, and that ye resist that captain, the flesh: *For that is all ye are able to do.*"

Holiness: A Co-operative Venture Between You and God

The last phrase in Luther's comment points out something which we can easily overlook. In the battle between flesh and Spirit, it is important to know what is expected of us. But it is equally important to know what is *not* expected of us. The latter is the point which is almost universally overlooked.

Philippians 2:12 says, "Work out your own salvation with fear and trembling..." This speaks of something we are to do. But the next verse says, "*For God is at work in you*, both to will and to work for his good pleasure." That speaks of what we cannot do; God must do it.

Christian growth is a co-operative work between the believer and God. Attempting to do what is not our part is as great an error as neglecting to do what is our part. Indeed, one of the Enemy's cleverest ploys is to goad us into doing that which is not expected of us—which, in fact, is impossible for us—and thereby to discourage us so that we end up not even doing that which is expected and is possible.

What is our part, and what is God's part in this co-operative venture? Two other passages of Scripture throw further light on the subject. Psalm 51:6-12: "Behold, thou desirest truth in the *inward being*; therefore teach me wisdom in my *secret heart*. Purge me with hyssop, and I shall be clean; wash me, and I shall be whiter than snow. Fill me with joy and gladness. ... Create in me a clean heart, O God, and put a new and right spirit within me. Cast me not away from thy presence, and take not thy holy Spirit from me. Restore to me the joy of thy salvation, and uphold me with a willing spirit."

Who acts in these verses, and who is acted upon? Who brings about "truth in the inward being . . . in the secret heart"? It is *God* who teaches, purges, washes, fills, creates, restores, and upholds. Whatever change takes place deep within the heart is the work of God.

Now, Colossians 3:12–14: "*Put on* then, as God's chosen ones, holy and beloved, compassion, kindness, lowliness, meekness, and patience, forbearing one another and, if one has a complaint against another, forgiving each other; as the Lord has forgiven you, so you also must forgive. And above all these, *put on* love, which binds everything together in perfect harmony."

Who acts in these verses? Who "puts on" compassion, kindness, lowliness, meekness, patience, forbearance, love? It is God's chosen ones; it is the believer. The outward, visible work of "putting on" is the work of the believer.

This, then, is the 'division of labour' in the work of sanctification: The believer puts on the outward form of Christ; God works the inward change in the heart.

Build the Forms—Let God Fill Them

Think of the wooden forms that a carpenter builds before cement is going to be poured. These forms describe the shape which the cement will take. When the cement hardens, they will be thrown away; only the cement will remain. They serve a temporary function, whereas the cement endures.

The wooden forms represent the believer's role in

sanctification. The believer does not himself work patience, kindness, or love into himself. He simply constructs the outward form into which God pours His enduring work of holiness.

Suppose a woman has a neighbour who tries her patience. She struggles to restrain her impatience. She clamps a lid on her smouldering resentments as best she can. But all the while she feels guilty because she is so impatient. "I just *have* to be more patient!" she keeps telling herself. But without success. She seems totally incapable of changing herself. And indeed she is. Impatience is an attitude of the heart. Only God can change it.

Now she comes to see the truth we are considering. She realizes that she is not expected to change her impatience to patience. She is simply expected to "put on" patience. She is to build the form which describes the outer shape of patience.

So she goes to her spiritual carpentry shop and selects some appropriate boards to build her form. The first one has *Listening* stamped on it. She will begin to listen to this irritating neighbour. True enough, the neighbour rarely listens to her. But that's not the point. She is not looking for any particular return from the neighbour. She is constructing a form into which God can pour His patience, and listening is one side of it. "Hear that neighbour out, get to know her a little better. Don't worry about how impatient you feel while you are listening. When the form is completed, and God pours in His patience, the impatience will be displaced as surely as cement displaces air when it is poured into a waiting form."

Prayer would be a second board in constructing this

form for patience. Perhaps you have never prayed for that neighbour. You begin to ask God's blessing upon her and her family.

Here's another board that fits well into the form: *A thoughtful deed*. Oh yes, she never volunteers to do anything for you. No matter. The board will help create the kind of form that God can use. So you offer to take care of her kids while she goes shopping, or you take her a little gift.

Then you close in the form with that board lying over in the corner, all covered with dust: *Kind comment*. You're not the only one whom this neighbour irritates. Get any group in the neighbourhood together, and you're likely to hear a slurring remark about her— the way she yells at her husband, or the way she raises her kids. So into such a conversation you drop a kind comment—something true, something praiseworthy.

The Place of FAITH

And now your form is complete—except for one thing. It isn't nailed together. You might have just the right boards, but if you don't nail them together, the cement will go running out and all the work of selecting the boards will be wasted. The nails that hold this spiritual form together are called faith.

But faith in what? *Faith that the form is going to be used*. In our figure, faith that the man with the cement is going to follow and pour his cement into the form which you have built.

Can you imagine a carpenter who builds forms all day long, but the man with the cement never comes along? Day in and day out he builds wooden forms, but they never get filled with cement. What pointless work!

Pointless also is the work of one who "puts on" the form of patience, love, or kindness *without the certain faith that God is going to use that form to do a work in the heart*. This whole work of sanctification depends upon faith—faith that when we construct the outward form, God will fill it with His divine cement.

The wooden forms which a carpenter builds are often a little ungainly. One board sticks out beyond the others. Two boards lying next to each other don't match well. Another is marred and gouged. And so it is with the forms of holiness which we construct. They are only an approximation of the real thing—the best approximation of outward conformity which we can come up with. But when we do this for God, in the faith that He will fill it, it serves His purpose. In due time the ungainly outer form will have served its purpose and can be discarded. Only the divine cement will remain.

The form which we construct—the patience which we "put on"—will never be as beautiful or true or strong as the real thing. It is not intended to be. It is simply our active expression of faith that God will form in us a patience which is beautiful and true and real.

This is what St. Paul is getting at in Galatians 5:16 when he says, "Do not *gratify* the desires of the flesh." He does not say, "Do not *have* the desires," but "do not *gratify* them." In other words. do not allow them outward expression.

The flesh stirs up a desire in you to strike out and hurt someone who has crossed your path. This verse does not tell you, "Now, you shouldn't feel that way; that's a terrible way for a Christian to feel!" It says simply, "Do not *gratify* that desire. Do not let that sarcastic word cross your lips. Do not let the fist strike out. Don't carry out that plan which would cause the other person hurt. Do not *gratify*."

As you build this outward form of non-gratification *in faith that God will fill it*, God takes the responsibility for replacing that desire of the flesh with the fruit of the Spirit. A simple and blessed co-operation: We do the outward and temporary work; God does the inward and lasting work.

What remains when all is done is God's workmanship. Sanctification is truly a work of grace. Yet we have had a part in it: Our faith has constructed a form which could *receive* His gracious work, for God does not pour out His grace where there is no faith to receive it.

This, then, is the secret of sanctification: *To construct the outward forms of holiness with expectant faith that God will fill them.*

The Importance of HONESTY

The thought may rise up: 'But doesn't this make us hypocrites?" If we say a kind word or do something thoughtful—when we *feel* just the opposite!—doesn't that make us hypocrites? No, it does not. A hypocrite is someone who pretends to be something he is not. But we don't kid ourselves. We are absolutely honest before God.

"Lord, You know that I don't have a speck of patience with that person. But, Lord, *I believe*—I believe that when I construct the outward form of patience, You will faithfully fill that form with patience which is truly divine. If You were not to do that, all my putting on would be so much wasted motion. It wouldn't create in me one iota of real patience. But, Lord, I trust You. I know that You *will* fill this outward form with the content of true patience! You will work in me 'that which is pleasing' in Your sight!" (Heb. 13:21).

These outward forms are built *unto the Lord*, not unto other people. There is no hypocrisy in presenting these outward forms of love as though we really mean them—for indeed we do! The only hypocrisy would be if we were to assume *before the Lord* that the outward forms constituted true holiness. So long as we clearly recognize and confess that these outward forms are merely the occasion or receptacle for God to do His enduring work in our hearts, there is no danger of hypocrisy.

What a load is lifted from our backs when we grasp this simple truth! No longer are we caught up in the hopeless (and indeed wicked) task of trying to bludgeon our heart into submission to *our* will.

"Be more loving!" we growl at ourselves. "And get gentle—do you hear me? Get gentle! And don't let me feel another unkind attitude coming from you, understand!"

All of that is quietly and with determination set aside. The whole inner work in the heart is turned completely over to God. We simply construct the outward forms of holiness, and let the heart be shaped according to His will, by His Spirit. *For the heart will not and cannot submit to our will. The heart can be changed only by the Holy Spirit.*

Free and Victorious Through Christ

We do not need to be enslaved to how we "feel", or to what we "want" at any given moment. We do not walk by our feelings or our wants: we walk by our faith. We believe that as we conform our lives to the will of God in all outward things, to the best of our ability, He will gradually conform our feelings and wants to coincide with Christ's feelings and wants.

We do not suppress or deny our feelings: we simply control their outward expression, while referring the feelings themselves to God. We come to look upon the desires of the flesh with a certain detached calm. For we *believe* that the divine cement of the Spirit will quietly and effectually displace that desire of the flesh in God's time. We may be a day—we may be a year— at building any given form. No matter. "The God of peace will himself sanctify you wholly ... He who calls you is faithful, and he will do it" (1 Thess. 5:23, 24).

Released from the slavery to how we feel, we are free to follow and fulfil God's plan for our life. A woman's magazine carried an article entitled, 'I Learned to Love My Husband". The author related how she had rushed into an early and unwise marriage just to get out of an unpleasant home situation. When the newness of the relationship wore off, she found herself trapped in marriage to a man whom she did not love.

Somehow this basic truth of sanctification came to her. She began to act the way a woman would act who *did* love her husband. She went to extra trouble cooking the foods he especially liked. She began to keep house to please him. She expressed herself towards him in the most loving ways she could.

Some years later one of their teenage children bore eloquent testimony to the success of this venture: "Mum, all the kids say we sure are lucky because you and Dad like each other so much." She had constructed the outward form of love—and God had faithfully filled it with the real thing!

God has programmed a plan of sanctification for every believer. He has a whole series of blueprints prepared for each one of us, in meaningful sequence. As we live close to Him, He will show us the blueprint for the next form we are to construct. And as we construct the forms of holiness which He sets out before us, and experience His divine filling, Ephesians 2:10 will become our personal experience of victory:

"For we are his workmanship, created in Christ Jesus for good works, which God prepared beforehand, that we should walk in them."

CHAPTER TWO

Explore the Mystery of God

When Jesus came into Galilee preaching "The time is fulfilled and the kingdom of God is at hand," He was not introducing a new idea to the people. He was touching on a hope that was deep-rooted in the heart of every Israelite. Their Scriptures and their traditions were saturated with it.

It was there in the visions of Daniel and Ezekiel and Zechariah. It was there in the prophecies of Isaiah and Jeremiah. It was there in the reigns of David and Solomon, seen as a type of God's coming kingdom. It was there in the word of the Lord on Mount Sinai, "You shall be to me a kingdom of priests and a holy nation" (Ex. 19:6). It was there in the parting blessing of aged Jacob upon the head of Judah, "The sceptre shall not depart from Judah, nor the ruler's staff from between his feet" (Gen. 49:10). It was there in the promise to Abraham, that he should possess a land and become a great nation (Gen. 12:1–2).

Through the years of the Old Testament, the idea of a coming Kingdom of God had been slowly unfolded and developed. In the day of Jesus it smouldered as a hope in the heart of every son of Israel—a hope of deliverance, a hope of establishment as a people—a hope of glory.

The Promise of a Kingdom

Jesus came to fulfil the promise of a kingdom. The first word spoken concerning Him was that "the Lord God will give to him the throne of his father David, and he will reign over the house of Jacob for ever; and of his kingdom there will be no end" (Luke 2:32). The last question put to Him on earth, before His ascension, was, "Lord, will you at this time restore the *kingdom* to Israel?" (Acts 1:6). His very designation as "Messiah" or "Christ" means "the Anointed One"—a kingdom designation, after the type of the anointing of kings in the Old Testament.

The "kingdom of his beloved Son", which Paul speaks about in Colossians 1:13, is the very Kingdom of God prophesied all through the Old Testament. The "hope of glory", which he speaks about in verse 27, is precisely the kingdom-hope which runs through both the Old and the New Testaments.

The Mystery of the Kingdom

The kingdom has about it a hidden element, a "mystery". The mystery was not revealed to previous ages and generations. Only in the wake of Christ's life–death–resurrection–ascension did God fully reveal this mysterious aspect of His kingdom. And the mystery is this: "*Christ IN you, the hope of glory*" (Col. 1:27). The essence of the Kingdom of God is contained in Christ, and Christ is in you. Christ—Christ *in* you—the glory for which you hope, is the kingdom. The Kingdom of God is not "here" or "there", Jesus said. "The kingdom of God is within you" (Luke 17:21).

A dreadful tendency within the Church has been to sentimentalize and rationalize this profound mystery of our faith. "The kingdom of God is within you" has been taken to mean that the kingdom consists of the moral and spiritual values which Jesus taught, which a person takes into himself through instruction, and by which he then tries to guide his life. But this is precisely what the kingdom is *not*—for then it would no longer be a "mystery" hidden from previous ages and generations.

The moral and spiritual values of the Kingdom of God were not hidden from previous ages and generations. They were spelled out in great detail. Jesus' teachings were largely quotations and applications of kingdom values already revealed in the Old Testament.

The mystery was not the moral and spiritual values which Jesus taught. The mystery was rather this totally unforeseen element: that the essence of the Kingdom of God would be summed up in the person of Christ, and that He would then be mysteriously imparted to believers through the power of the Holy Spirit.

What is the great lack in our daily walk as Christians? Why the frustration in our desire to live a holy life? Why the lack of power? Is it not this, that we are still living in the shadow of Mount Sinai, trying to live a God-pleasing life by the power of our own will and good intentions, rather than by the power of the indwelling Christ? We have not entered into the mystery of the kingdom.

A Parable: The Salvation Saloon

A young man named Sinner once received from his Father a beautiful, bright-red Salvation Saloon. It was sparkling new, and it delighted the young man's heart, the more so because it was a gift.

"I did nothing whatever to earn it," the young man exulted. "He just gave it to me. Why, I couldn't have saved enough money to buy a car like this if I'd worked for years and years. It was a gift—a sheer gift!" Indeed, so delighted was he with his new red car that he changed his own name to be more like it—from Sinner to Saved.

He polished his car every day. He took pictures of it to send to his friends and relatives. He looked it over from front to back. He even crawled underneath to admire its excellent workmanship. He never tired of telling those who came along, "My Father gave it to me—a free gift!"

Some days later the young man was seen out on the highway, pushing his bright red car. A slender man came up, introduced himself as Mr. Helper, and asked if he might be of assistance.

"Oh, thank you," the young man said, panting a little. "I'm doing just fine! I had a little trouble at first because the bumper kept cutting into my hands—especially on the hills. But then a man helped me—a wonderful man, a specialist on car bodies—he showed me how you can mount little rubber cushions right here on the underside of the bumper—and then you can push for hours and hours without even a blister!"

Mr. Helper nodded. "Yes, I can see that those rubber cushions would be a help."

"And I've been trying out something new which I heard some people are using," the young man continued with some enthusiasm. "You put your *back* against the car, flex your knees, and then lift, at a 45-degree angle. It works like a charm, especially on muddy roads."

"Yes," Mr. Helper agreed, "I can see how that would help—would give you more leverage."

"That's it! It's the leverage that does it. And then, too, it's a good change—sort of a relaxation from straight-ahead pushing."

"Have you pushed the car quite a way?" Mr. Helper asked.

"Oh yes, more than 200 miles since I got it," the young man said proudly.

"It's a beautiful car," Mr. Helper admitted.

The young man's eyes lit up. "It was a gift, you know. My Father gave it to me—a free gift."

Mr. Helper nodded, without speaking. He walked around the car, looking in the windows. After a time he said, "It must be quite tiring, pushing a big car like this."

"Yes, it is," the young man admitted with a manly sigh. "But, then, it's a wonderful thing to get tired for, isn't it, a free gift from my Father? The least I can do is push it!" Some of the enthusiasm had drained from his voice, but he still managed to smile.

Mr. Helper opened the left door of the bright red car and said, "Won't you get in and sit down?"

The young man drew back uncertainly. He glanced into the car. It seemed a little, well, a little presumptuous for a person to get inside the car. He knew that there *was* an inside, but certainly you would never get anywhere if you *used* it. Yet, after a moment's hesitation, he decided that perhaps it would be all right to just slide in and sit down. He had stopped to rest anyway, and nothing really depended on it. He slid into the seat, holding himself erect, not quite daring to relax against the backrest.

Mr. Helper walked around, opened the other door, and slid in behind the steering wheel. He touched the starter button, and moments later they were speeding down the highway at 50 miles an hour.

The young man was quite breathtaken. He found the ride pleasant—even a bit exciting! But it seemed unorthodox, somehow. He knew that you must have a red Salvation Saloon to be admitted through the gate at the end of the highway. But *getting* it there, well, that was *his* responsibility, wasn't it . . . ?

Saved by Faith—Sanctified by Faith

This parable portrays the state of a good many Christians. They are quite straight on the issue of justification—it is a free gift, all of grace. But sanctification is still being carried on by self-effort. We have been taught that the Holy Spirit works in us; but our deep, inward reliance is still too much upon what *we* must do to become holy, what *we* must do to build the kingdom. We are pushing the car by our own efforts. The indwelling of Christ is little more than a mental concept, another name for conscience, telling us when and where and how fast we must push the car.

But Christ does not indwell us in order to play the part of conscience, to be "on hand" so He can tell us what to do. He indwells us in order that He himself might do in us and through us the Father's good pleasure. Sanctification is not a matter of doing God's will by our own effort, but of the life of Christ, which dwells within us, being released to do God's will.

How is it done? By *faith*. In Colossians 2:6, Paul says, "As you *received* Christ Jesus the Lord, so *live* in him." The power of God *for* us (Christ's atonement) was only released as we trusted Him for it, as we had faith; likewise, the power of Christ *in* us can only be released as we exercise faith. As surely as we are *saved* by faith, we are *sanctified* by faith. As surely as *salvation* is solely the work of Christ, just as surely is *sanctification* solely the work of Christ.

What a joy! What a release! As a condemned sinner you came to Jesus and said, "Lord, I confess my sin and my utter inability to cleanse myself of guilt. Wash me in Your blood, and reconcile me with the Father." And He did it, simply because you gave up trying to justify yourself, and trusted Him to do it for you. He saved you. And now, as a child of God, reconciled to the Father by the blood of Christ, you come to Jesus and say, "Lord, You see how weak I am, how unlike You; how lacking in every grace; how quick to criticize others, how slow to recognize fault in myself; how ready to clutch glory; how eager for my own pleasure. Make me like yourself." And He does it. As soon as you give up trying to sanctify yourself and trust Him to work sanctification in you, His indwelling life is released. The "hope of glory" comes into manifestation.

Works: Not for God, but for Us

To know this profound mystery of our faith that Christ, the hope of Kingdom glory, is within us, waiting the consent of faith so that His life can be released—to know this puts the whole matter of "good works" in a new perspective. We have been accustomed to think of good works as something which we do for God, out of gratitude for the gift of salvation. But now we recognize in every good work a God-created opportunity for the indwelling life of Christ to be further released.

A good work is not something which we do for God, but rather it is something which God has created beforehand for us (Eph. 2:11). A good work functions as a catalyst to further release the life of Christ, and conform us to His image. God's ultimate concern in regard to a good work is not what we do, but what the work does to us. A good work contributes to the kingdom only as it becomes an event which releases the life of Christ within us. In so far as some good to others may result from this, that is a sovereign work of God for which to praise Him yet more!

In our church we once built a prayer chapel. There were different ideas as to how it should be designed and used, some of them quite contrary to one another. In this simple undertaking, God created a wonderful opportunity for the life of Christ to be released in our midst, to demonstrate how Jesus can mould unity of understanding and purpose. It was not that we built a building for God, but rather He graciously created a good work for us to do, in order that something of Jesus might rub off on us as we built and used it.

A good work is always an opportunity for something of Jesus to rub off on us. It is not so much our response to God's grace, as it is yet a further expression of His grace towards us. The chapels and churches and missions we build will one day pass away. And when we stand before the Father, He will not be judging our "works"—the chapels and churches and missions we've built—but He will be judging us, *according to our works*, looking to see how much of Jesus was formed in us as we walked in these good works which He prepared beforehand (Eph. 2:11).

This means that we are not free to pick our good works at random, and charge into them with the banner of good intentions flying high. The works must be ones which God has prepared beforehand. He prepares works which are particularly suited to our situation, stage of growth, and future ministry—works which in their very makeup will provide maximum opportunity for the life of Christ to be released.

This is the "mystery", hidden for ages and generations, but now revealed to us, His saints: That we can stop longing for the Kingdom of God, stop struggling to gain it or build it—it is ours. The glory of the Kingdom of God has been summed up in Christ, and Christ is *in you*!

CHAPTER THREE

Discover the Secret of Sanctification

Imagine a ten-chapter book on marriage which spends nine chapters covering the details of the wedding ceremony, then in the final chapter whisks through such things as the following:

1. Getting adjusted to one another
2. Managing finances
3. Raising children
4. Resolving differences
5. Relationships with in-laws
6. Planning for the children's education
7. Investing wisely for retirement
8. Moving into old age

Anyone who has been married longer than a few weeks would sense that something here is badly out of balance. Important as it is to *get* married, it takes a lot more grace and "learn-how" to *stay* happily married.

The same kind of observation has been made about the Christian life: It takes a 5% input to become a Christian, but a 95% input to live as a Christian—to grow and develop into the kind of a Christian God wants us to be. Yet the emphasis in the church, especially in the Protestant church, has sometimes been about as unbalanced as our imaginary book on marriage: We spend 95% of our time talking about "getting saved".

Because of Christ's death on the Cross, God forgives our sin, accounts us righteous, and gives us eternal life. The technical word is justification. It's the wedding ceremony. It unites us to Christ.

This great and wonderful truth (for it *is* great and wonderful) we discuss and analyse and preach about and discourse upon for nine chapters at least. Then we dash off one quick chapter at the end in which we say, "So let's live a good Christian life to show God how grateful we are for the gift of salvation and eternal life..."

More Than Gratitude

Gratitude becomes the great motivation for the Christian life. There is truth in this. But it needs to be examined. For it can involve us in a subtle form of works-righteousness. If the Christian life is a "striving born of gratitude", as Kierkegaard has said, then too easily we can find ourselves paying for our salvation—on the instalment plan! Saved now—pay later. You get justified by faith right now on the spot. But the rest of your life you find yourself clipping out gratitude coupons and pasting them in your payment book. The only difference between you and the Pharisees is a certain theory of salvation. Your everyday life is largely unaffected by this great salvation you talk about. You're just as much bound by good works as the person who is trying to accumulate enough merit to pay for his salvation outright.

Sanctification involves something else than a striving born of gratitude. It is a life not only begun in faith but continued in faith. "As therefore you received Christ Jesus the Lord [i.e., by faith], so *live* in him" (Col. 2:6). It is precisely this failure to continue in faith which causes problems in the area of sanctification. "Having begun with the Spirit, are you now ending with the flesh?" (Gal. 3:3).

We have assumed too much about sanctification. "Once we are saved," so it is assumed, "obviously we know how to live a good Christian life!" That's like assuming that once two people have exchanged vows at the altar, then *obviously* they know how to build a good marriage! Divorce statistics tell another story. And likewise, the number of Christians who have made a genuine decision for Christ, and then fallen away from it, tell a similar sad story of frustration and failure.

The WHAT and the HOW of Sanctification

In 1 Thessalonians 5:14–22, the Apostle Paul lays down quite a catalogue for sanctification:

1. *Respect* your spiritual superiors.
2. *Be patient* with those under you.
3. *Do good* to all, even if they haven't deserved it.
4. *Rejoice* always.
5. *Pray* constantly.
6. *Give thanks* under all circumstances.
7. *Encourage* the spirit.
8. *Encourage* prophecy.
9. *Test* all things.
10. *Abstain* from evil.

Whew! Difficult to *remember* all that, to say nothing of doing it!

This is the typical approach to sanctification. It begins by telling you what the Christian life involves—what you should and should not do. The problem comes if we end the chapter there. We stop with the *what*, and never get on to the really crucial question, the *how*. Most of us have some notion of what the Christian life asks of us. The one commandment, "love your neighbour as yourself", would keep us going for a long time. But the thing we stumble over is *how? How* can I do it?

The Apostle Paul doesn't end his chapter with the *what*. He goes on to reveal one of the great truths of sanctification : "May the God of peace himself sanctify you wholly; and may your spirit and soul and body be kept sound and blameless at the coming of our Lord Jesus Christ. He who calls you is faithful, and he will do it" (1 Thess. 5:23, 24).

There it is, the secret of sanctification : The God of peace *Himself* will sanctify. The One who called you to this life *will do it*!

Sanctification is not merely a command—it is a *promise*. It is not merely a roster of duties set before us; it is the promise that God, by His Holy Spirit, will work all these things in us. Thus it is not merely my *will* which is involved, but my *faith*—my *trust*.

Looking at that list of duties which the Apostle enumerates, we could visualize ourselves stumbling after project 2 or 3 or 7 or 10. But the promise is : He will sanctify you *wholly*. He is faithful. He will do it. If we are willing in our weakness to be obedient, He is willing in His strength to see that we can be obedient.

The Secret: God Works It in You

This is the glorious secret of sanctification. Underlying the commands of God is the promise of God that *he* will do it. The Christian life is not just a list of well-meaning religious exercises. It is a new full-time attitude of heart. It is, in the language of the Bible, a death-and-resurrection.

The story is told of Martin Luther one day answering a knock at his door. "Does Dr. Martin Luther live here?" the man asked. "No," Luther answered, "he died. Christ lives here now."

What expectancy—what a sense of adventure—this brings into one's Christian experience! Where before you looked to your own talents and abilities and resources, now you look at the good work God has set before you, and you reckon upon the limitless resources of Christ Jesus!

"Lord, I haven't a *thing* to bring this woman who has just lost her husband, but I know that *You* do. Lord, You know what a problem I have, brooding over past mistakes: I wonder how You're going to work that out of me. Lord, we see how You've been working a deeper concern in us for the Jewish people in the community: We look to You to open the door of witness at the right time and in the right way."

One man carried this yet a step further. He said, "And if things go sour—if I 'muff the ball' well, that's His problem too. I'm His child, His problem child, and this sanctification business is *His* business!"

We do "muff the ball" in the Christian life. And when we do, we *can* turn to Him and say, "Here I am, Lord, your problem child!" This is not the language of flippancy. It is the language of trust, which does not leave room for the devil, but trusts the loving Father to work the problem out of His problem child!

Look at that list of commands again: Do good; rejoice; pray; give thanks; encourage; test; abstain, etc.! Only now it does not seem so utterly impossible. Because we have a new notion of the *how*. It doesn't depend on us or on the resources we are able to muster. It depends on Jesus, who calls us. He is faithful, and He will do it!

Christ does not indwell us in order to tell us what we "ought to do", in our own natural strength, but to convert the burdensome and impossible "ought" into a glorious "It shall be so!" By the power of His life it shall be so!

A man found himself in a working relationship with a woman who had a whole arsenal of irritating habits. He struggled with all his thought and willpower to hold his patience, love her, understand her, be charitable towards her. But the most he could muster was a thinly disguised politeness. Then one morning, in desperation, he said, "Lord, I can't even *like* that woman! If You want her to be loved. You'll have to do it through me." And from that moment there began to flow into his thoughts and words and actions a new power that touched the life of that woman in a most remarkable way, to the extent that even other people began to wonder "what had got hold of her".

As long as he was trying to do it in his own power and out of his own resources, he failed miserably. When his own talents for love and patience were willing to die, the life that is in Christ Jesus sprang to life.

Jesus said, "Unless a grain of wheat falls into the

earth and dies, it remains alone; but if it dies; it bears much fruit" (John 12:24). The secret of a fruitful Christian life is not in *doing* but in *dying*—dying to all self-effort, so that the indwelling life of Christ can be released.

This is the secret of sanctification, which includes gratitude, but goes beyond it. It makes of the Christian life not a duty but an adventure. Each day you can wake up and say, "Lord, what have You planned for today?" Not what am I going to do for the Lord, but what is He going to do with me?

> O gracious God, wilt Thou my heart
> So fashion in each secret part,
> That Thou be sanctified in me,
> Till Thee in heaven above I see,
> Where holy, holy, holy Lord,
> We sing to Thee with sweet accord!

PART TWO: THE RENEWED MIND FACES CHALLENGES WITH THE AUTHORITY OF CHRIST

THE OLD LANDLORD
UNILATERAL FORGIVENESS

CHAPTER FOUR

The Old Landlord

Think of yourself as living in a block of flats. You live there under a landlord who has made your life miserable. He charges you exorbitant rent. When you can't pay, he loans you money at a fearful rate of interest, to get you even further into his debt. He barges into your flat at all hours of the day and night, wrecks and dirties the place up, then charges you extra for not maintaining the premises. Your life is miserable.

Then comes Someone who says, "I've taken over this block of flats. I've purchased it. You can live here as long as you like, free. The rent is paid up. I am going to be living here with you, in the manager's flat."

What a joy! You are saved! You are delivered out of the clutches of the old landlord!

But what happens? You hardly have time to rejoice in your new-found freedom, when a knock comes at the door. And there he is—the old landlord! Mean, glowering, and demanding as ever. He has come for the rent, he says.

What do you do? Do you pay him? Of course you don't! Do you go out and pop him on the nose? No—he's bigger than you are!

You confidently tell him, "You'll have to take that

up with the new Landlord." He may bellow, threaten, wheedle, and cajole. You just quietly tell him, "Take it up with the new Landlord." If he comes back a dozen times, with all sorts of threats and arguments, waving legal-looking documents in your face, you simply tell him yet once again, "Take it up with the new Landlord." In the end he has to. He knows it, too. He just hopes that he can bluff and threaten and deceive you into doubting that the new Landlord will really take care of things.

Now this is the situation of a Christian. Once Christ has delivered you from the power of sin and the devil, you can depend on it: that old landlord will soon come back knocking at your door. And what is your defence? How do you keep him from getting the whip hand over you again? You send him to the new Landlord. *You send him to Jesus.*

A Personal Testimony

When this first broke in upon me, I was out mowing the lawn. Suddenly I realized the implication of this simple truth: If Christ has set me free, then I am free *indeed*! I don't have to entertain all the negative impressions that come knocking at the door of my mind. I don't have to let that old landlord come barging in, waving all his bills in my face. So I consciously claimed my deliverance in Christ, and then I waited.

Sure enough, the old landlord was right there, knocking at the door. The thought came into my mind: "When are you going to find time for any reading and studying when the autumn programme begins at church? You are going to be snowed under!" But now

I realized that this wasn't my thought. This was a thought which was trying to infiltrate my mind, get me to accept it, so it could hold a club over my head. This was the old landlord trying to collect from me a bill marked "Worry."

"You'll have to take that up with Jesus," I told him.

He began to enumerate a few more details, telling me how impossible the autumn schedule was going to be. But I told him again, "That may all be true, but will you take it up with Jesus, please?" He went reluctantly. He knew I was right. "Cast all your anxieties on him, for he cares about you" (1 Pet. 5:7).

He didn't stay away long. He was back a few moments later.

"Say, I want to come in and talk with you about those people that have been telling lies about you." He had a nice friendly smile on his face. He oozed concern. But I saw what he had behind his back: A big fat bill marked "Self-pity".

"Take it up with Jesus," I told him.

"They may get you in real trouble!" His voice took on a little edge, and I saw that he had another bill lurking behind his back marked "Fear".

The same answer: "Take it up with Jesus." That's the way I handle temptation now. Not willpower, not strength of character, not making a flock of resolutions. Just: "Take it to Jesus."

The old landlord must have come back a couple of hundred times that first hour, while I was out mowing the lawn. I never realized before what a playground for Satan our minds can become. But here's the point, and the power: *we don't have to let him in!* Christ has delivered us, really delivered us. When these thoughts

come knocking at the door of our mind, we can quietly
send them on to Jesus.

Don't argue with them. That's letting them get one
foot in the door. (That was Eve's trouble—she got into
a conversation with the tempter.) Before the conversation even gets under way, quietly and confidently say,
"Take that up with Jesus."

Four Practical Tips

1. *Don't let your feelings fool you.* Feelings are one
of the old landlord's strongest weapons. When he
waves these things in your face, it will stir up all the
old feelings you had before Christ delivered you—fear,
doubt, guilt, lust, anxiety, despair. The old feelings will
be right there, and strong. Don't be afraid of them.
Simply do not follow them. Rather, just quietly tell
that thought, "Take the whole matter up with Jesus."
It may take some persistence on your part, but eventu-
ally he will leave. He has to. You have the Name of
Power.

When Christ sets you free, it's like pulling a big
weed out by the roots. There are little troughs left in
the earth, where the roots used to be. These don't
cover over at once. So what does the Enemy do? He
beams a thought into your mind. He lays it right in the
trough where the old root used to be—right where the
memories are still easily aroused, right where the feelings that used to accompany that thing still lie raw and
exposed. The memories stir up, the feelings are in-
flamed. Your faith in Christ faces a practical test. Are
you going to trust the Word and promise of God, even
despite your thoughts and feelings?

Remember the simple rule: *Feelings follow faith*. The old landlord cannot stay around forever. When he leaves, your feelings will subside.

2. *Do not become discouraged by the frequency or the repetition of the same temptation*. Repetition is another of the old landlord's favourite weapons. We might resist him two, three, four times, but then we become weary. He convinces us that we are, after all, still as undelivered as ever. So we open the door and let him in.

If the same thought comes back a hundred times in the same day, a hundred times quietly and confidently send it on to Jesus. And rejoice! Yes, *rejoice*! Because the old landlord cannot come knocking one more time than he gets permission from God to do so.

Read the book of Job and see: Before Satan ever moved against Job, he had to get permission from God to do so. God lets the old landlord come knocking. This is the way in which your faith is built up. Every time you send the old landlord on to Jesus, your faith in your Deliverer is strengthened. And if he knocks loud and bellows fiercely, and if he returns a hundred, yes, a thousand times, rejoice! For with every encounter— with every turning him away to Jesus—you are being knit in trust and faith to your Deliverer.

3. *Do not feel that this requires some kind of super-human willpower*. This whole way of victory in Jesus is not based on willpower at all: It is based on faith— faith in the reality and authority of Jesus.

Consider again our illustration: Suppose the old landlord comes knocking at the door when the father and mother of the family have gone to the store. The five-year-old daughter is home alone. He blusters out his usual threats and demands. In herself the child has no "strength". She is just a five-year-old. But she is prepared. She knows the way things really stand.

By no strength of her own, but purely because of the incontestable authority of the new Landlord, she says calmly and confidently, "You'll have to take that up with the new Landlord." No fear. No shouting. No struggle. No "willpower". *Just simple trust and confidence (the Bible calls it "faith") in an incontestable authority.* That is what you have in Jesus: An Incontestable Authority. "*All* authority in heaven and on earth has been given to me" (Matt. 28:18).

4. *Cut your conversation with the old landlord short.* In effect, give him to understand that you have other important things to do! For instance, you can turn to Jesus in an act of worship, song, or praise. This guards against the danger of this whole thing becoming just a "new law"—a routine which you follow, more-or-less successfully, but one which does not really build up your personal relationship to Jesus.

Imagine the case of a man who has had a habit of lust. He cannot sit down at a lunch counter without casting a furtive, lusting glance at the waitress. He never goes by a news-stand without paging through some lurid book or magazine. Even in his relations with his wife, there is more of lust than real love.

Then he is saved. He receives the life of Jesus, and he knows that he cannot continue to do this sort of thing. But he does not understand this life of deliverance-through-Jesus. So he merely applies the law. He tries to "contain" this lust of the flesh by resolve and will-power. He has a measure of success, but also many a failure. And in none of this is he really bound to Jesus in love. In fact, he may even begin inwardly to resent the hard life Jesus calls him to, and excuse himself a little lusting.

But now he learns this life of deliverance. He sees a lewd magazine on a bus station rack. He does not "fight" against this temptation. He does not simply grit his teeth and suffer through the duration of this temptation, saying over and over to himself, "I will not lust, I will not lust, I will not lust." Evil resisted grows stronger. "The power of sin is the *law*" (1 Cor. 15:56). The more he invokes the law against his lusting, the more powerful grows the sin within him. He has tried that method before, and failed.

The way of real deliverance lies in quite another direction. He sees the lewd magazine. He quietly recognizes within himself that this is a situation of temptation. *At once he takes up his impregnable position in* Christ *through an act of conscious worship*. He averts his eyes from the immediate source of temptation and inwardly begins to *praise Jesus*. Perhaps he sings a hymn to himself. He praises his wonderful *Deliverer*. Not in a fearful spirit, as though the lust at any moment might break through the door. (He has sent it on to Jesus, and it has to leave!) He praises Jesus in a joyful, confident spirit knowing that He, Jesus, has won the victory over lust. His authority cannot be challenged.

As he binds himself to Jesus in this conscious act of worship, the temptation will retreat. It is not the law which has saved him. He has simply yielded the whole thing to Jesus, through an act of worship.

Another thing you can do is enter into a preconceived plan of intercession. A man once found himself afflicted by blasphemous thoughts. He fought against them with all the resources of his conscious will, but to no avail. Then he struck on a different approach. He determined that whenever these blasphemous thoughts came knocking at the door of his mind, he would begin praying for his cousin Henry, a missionary in China. It was not long before the old landlord quit bringing that blasphemy bill around for collection, for he found that all it did was stir up a lot of prayer for China!

Turning to some routine job is another way to excuse yourself from a conversation with the old landlord. A good stint of garden work, or taking care of some long-needed repairs around the house, has frustrated the old landlord's plans more than once.

It is important to realize that the old landlord may tell you the "truth". Some of those bills *are* due— worry, hate, lust, laziness, pride. But that is not the point. The point is that *Jesus is now handling the matter*. The bills must be taken to Him for collection. He has paid the debt and set you free!

The Principle Behind It

This encounter with the old landlord is based on sound biblical principles—

1. *"Sin will have no dominion over you, since you are not under law but under grace"* (Rom 6 : 14).

Does this mean that our spiritual life becomes lawless and disorderly? "God forbid!" says St. Paul. To live under grace does not mean to live contrary to law. It means that you are now operating under a different regime in the battle against sin.

One of the prime responsibilities of a government is

to protect its citizens from coming under the dominion of any foreign power. When you live under the regime of the law, and sin mounts a siege of temptation against you, you start a counter-barrage of "Thou shalts" and "Thou shalt nots." You hurl them with all your might, but after a time you become weary. Sin outlasts you and gains dominion over you.

When God transfers you to the regime of grace, you no longer depend upon the law to defend you against an onslaught of temptation. You are under a regime with much more sophisticated weapons. Not the weapons of law, which you must wield in your own strength and determination, but the weapons of grace, which Christ himself puts into operation. When you learn to call upon the power of Christ, sin will not gain dominion over you.

2. *"Do not be conformed to this world, but be transformed by the renewal of your mind"* (Rom. 12 : 2).

The mind that is conformed to this world pays endless tribute to the old landlord. The renewed mind sets its faith and hope and trust and love upon Jesus. It "leads every thought captive to obey Christ" (2 Cor. 10 : 5). "Take it to Jesus" and "Praise be to Thee, O Lord" become the obbligato of one's life. And in this life of trust, we are transformed into the image of our Deliverer.

So if the old landlord comes and calls you a terrible sinner, you simply tell him, "Take it to Jesus." If he comes and stirs up feelings of hatred, resentment, or despair within you, you tell him once again, "Take it to Jesus." If he whispers in your ear that you did a marvellous job, and begins to inflate your ego, you tell him the same thing, "Take it to Jesus."

If he comes to you with the whip of the law and says, "You have to be more loving! You have to be more patient! You have to be more honest!" Remember, Christ is the end of the law, also. You tell him, "Take that to Jesus. Whatever good is to be worked in me will come through His Spirit, not through the law." And, with each encounter, you turn to Jesus in praise and adoration.

3. *"As therefore you received Christ Jesus the Lord, so live in him"* (Col. 2 : 6).

The faith that brought Jesus into your life is the faith by which you live. He is all-sufficient. He is the Alpha and the Omega, the beginning and the end. You wake up in the morning. The cares of the day begin to crowd in upon you. You send them on to Jesus. You go through the day facing the temptations and frustrations and problems of everyday life. One by one you refer them to Jesus. The life of inner warfare is transformed into a life of restful abiding in Christ. He is your Deliverer. He is, moment by moment, your ever sure defence.

Do you wonder whether such a life of faith and victory is possible? Do you find a little corner of doubt in your mind that says, "Perhaps for some this might be true, but surely not for me"? Send that doubt on to Jesus, and you will see!

CHAPTER FIVE

Unilateral Forgiveness

So far as the Scriptures tell us, no one ever came to Jesus and asked to be forgiven. There's much talk about forgiveness, and yet Jesus, the very fountainhead of forgiveness, never had one person come to Him and say, "Lord, forgive me". Yet He did forgive people. He forgave them in a very special way. He forgave them unilaterally.

"Unilateral" means "one-sided". Unilateral forgiveness is a forgiveness which flows out from the forgiver. The other person does not ask for it, may not even realize that he needs it. The forgiver *takes the initiative* and forgives without waiting for the other person to come and ask for forgiveness.

Four men brought their paralysed friend to Jesus. Jesus looked at him, and before they ever said a word He said, "My son, be of good cheer, your sins are forgiven" (Matt. 9:2). The man didn't ask for it. It went out from the Forgiver without any request being made. Jesus forgave the man unilaterally.

Jesus was visiting in the house of Simon the Pharisee. A woman who had a reputation as a sinner came in. She washed His feet with her tears and wiped them with her hair. Jesus said, "Go in peace, your sins are forgiven" (Luke 7:48). She didn't ask to be forgiven. The forgiveness went out from Jesus unilaterally.

The most gripping example of all comes as Jesus hangs on the Cross. "Father, forgive them, for they know not what they do." Those Roman soldiers did not beg, "Jesus of Nazareth, forgive us. We know You are a just and good man, but we have to do our duty, we have our orders." Yet the forgiveness went out to them from Jesus, unilaterally.

Jesus Gave This Power to the Church

After the resurrection, Jesus came to His disciples and said, " 'As the Father has sent me, even so I send you!' And when He had said this he breathed on them and said to them, 'Receive the Holy Spirit. If you forgive the sins of any, they are forgiven; if you retain the sins of any, they are retained' " (John 20:21-23). The initiative is with the disciples. It is unilateral forgiveness. It is the greatest power that Jesus left His Church. He meant it to be an on-going practice. Where the Church has practised this lesson, she has been unconquerable. Where she has failed to practise it, she has been divided and defeated, a spectacle of shame before men and angels.

We are all familiar with the prophetic approach to sin: The prophet points out specific sins, and calls people to repentance. This is what Nathan did when he came to David after his sin with Bathsheba. He said, "You are the man." David came to repentance, which is recorded in Psalm 51: "Against thee, thee only, have I sinned, and done that which is evil in thy sight."

The prophetic approach to sin hits every one of us at

certain times in our lives. It may come through the Bible, through a sermon, through reading, through listening to the radio, or through the well-chosen word of a friend. You are called to repentance by a word of God that points out a specific sin in your life.

But there is another way, this way of unilateral forgiveness, which proceeds out from the one who forgives. Sin is not only something which brings guilt upon us. Sin also manifests itself as *power*. There are people so bound by the power of sin that they literally cannot take hold of forgiveness. That is why unilateral forgiveness is essential in the Church.

Karl Barth, the Swiss theologian, said that sin never really burns the conscience until it comes under the white-hot light of forgiveness. We have tended to think according to just one pattern: conviction-repentance-forgiveness. But it can be otherwise: unilateral forgiveness-repentance-cleansing.

Paul tells us in Ephesians, "Let all bitterness and wrath and anger and clamour and slander be put away from you, with all malice, and be kind to one another, tenderhearted, forgiving one another, as God in Christ forgave you" (Eph. 4 : 31–32). And how did God in Christ forgive us? "God shows his love for us in that while we were *yet sinners* Christ died for us" (Rom. 5 : 8). The act of forgiveness preceded the act of repentance. The love and forgiveness of God is the light that breaks in upon our darkness and makes us realize our need.

There is a beautiful type of this in the Old Testament. On the Day of Atonement, two goats were brought to the high priest. The first goat was the sacrificial lamb. It was slaughtered and its blood sprinkled upon the altar as atonement for sin. Then, *after the forgiveness*, the high priest laid his hands on the second goat—the Scapegoat. He confessed all the sins of Israel on to the head of the Scapegoat. The animal was then driven into the wilderness, carrying away all the sins which had already been forgiven. The confession had the effect of "carrying the sins away". And it followed forgiveness.

Where the Church has practised unilateral forgiveness among its membership, and towards those who might persecute her from the outside, she has been unconquerable. This victory through unilateral forgiveness was experienced by Corrie ten Boom who had been imprisoned in a concentration camp by the Germans. Ten years after her ordeal in prison, she came face to face with the woman who had been a nurse in the hospital barracks where she and her sister Betsie were prisoners. Betsie was dying, and this nurse had been cruel to her in her helplessness. Corrie ten Boom says, "At that moment of recognition, hatred came into my heart. I thought I had overcome it, but now I saw her again after all these years, and great bitterness was in my heart. Ashamed, I confessed my guilt. 'Forgive me for my hatred, O Lord. Teach me to love my enemies.'"

She goes on to tell of praying for this enemy, finally of phoning her and inviting her to a meeting. She concludes: "The whole evening she listened and looked straight into my eyes. I knew that she listened with her heart. After the meeting I read with her from the Bible the way of salvation. 1 John 4:9 clinched the matter: 'In this was manifested the love of God towards us, because that God sent His only begotten Son into the

world, that we might live through Him.' She made the
decision that causes angels to rejoice. Not only had my
hatred gone, but I could shine into her dark heart: His
channel for streams of living water. . . ."

The world can never break the Church. The power
of hell cannot break the Church. The only thing that
can break the Church is her own unwillingness to live
in forgiveness. She must exercise this power that Christ
himself demonstrated.

In the very first martyrdom, Stephen reacted with
unilateral forgiveness: "I see the Son of Man standing
at the right hand of God . . . Father do not lay this sin
to their charge." Hebrews tells us that Jesus sat down
at the right hand of God (Heb. 1 : 3). But when Stephen
saw Him, He was *standing up*. David du Plessis says,
"Jesus stood up to honour Stephen and his word of unilateral forgiveness."

Picture the Lord, standing up, looking over the para-
pet of heaven, saying, "Who is this that my servant is
forgiving? I must go to that man." Yes, and go to that
man He did—to the ringleader of that band, Saul of
Tarsus. He met him on the road to Damascus. He met
him because Stephen had unilaterally forgiven him,
and opened the gateway for an encounter with Jesus.
And what a meeting that was! What blessings issued
from it! That is the kind of power which Jesus has
given His Church.

Unilateral Forgiveness—
The Key to Our Own Forgiveness

Our own forgiveness depends upon our willingness to
forgive others. "Forgive and you will be forgiven"

(Luke 7 : 37). As you forgive, God is able to forgive you. "Forgive if you have anything against anyone ... so that your Father also may forgive you your trespasses" (Mark 11 : 25). If we do not unilaterally forgive those against whom we have anything at all, God's hands are tied. He can't forgive us.

It is not natural to forgive people who are in the wrong, to forgive them unilaterally. The natural human response is to demand justice. Oh, if they would come to us and repent, we would forgive them. Yes, we'd be big about it! But to forgive unilaterally, the way Jesus did, when they don't even think they need to be forgiven—that rubs us the wrong way.

Mary Welch, with her keen insight into the Christian experience of love and forgiveness, writes in *The Golden Key* about a woman who had been maligned and slandered by certain church people who had great influence in the community. "They had called her 'good' evil. For seven years she couldn't pray or read her Bible. She hated the whole community for what they had done to her. Finally, she turned to drink."

All of that time the woman was willing to forgive. "But," Miss Welch continues, "she made her grave mistake at one point. She thought that forgiveness must wait for confession and apology from the offenders! So she had waited and suffered and hated—waiting for at least one fellow human being to come and confess that he had misunderstood or misinterpreted her—waiting so she could forgive and be rid of the heavy burden of resentment and hate. But nobody came. . . ."

Finally, through faith and obedience to Christian counsel, this woman drew a map of the town; going in imagination over every part of it, removing her judgment and sending forth blessing, thanking God for all that each person had ever done for or against her.

"She found freedom in giving freedom to those she had bound. She found life in giving room for God in every person she had held imprisoned in her judgment because they could be so small as to speak ill of her. So far as I know, to this day not a single person in her community has confessed or apologized to her for the wrong they committed against her. She has never had to tell a single one that he was forgiven and nobody had been embarrassed. But the whole community loves her and gives itself to her."

Don't be the judge. God has not made us judges of one another, but forgivers of one another. "If you judge one another," Paul says, "beware lest you devour one another" (Gal. 5 : 15).

In the history of the Church, if you look at every difficulty or division, at the root of the problem you will find an unwillingness to forgive unilaterally. On the other hand, where you find strength and power in the Church, you will find people who have learned this simple secret of forgiveness that does not depend upon what the other person says or does, but is a unilateral outflowing of the love of Christ.

Some may fear that this blanks out personal responsibility. What it actually does is open the door for God to really deal with a person. Whether that person receives the forgiveness—whether he accepts it, lives in it, moves on—that we cannot tell. Our part is to forgive, freely and without waiting to be asked.

Think of someone you have something against. Don't think about whether he deserves to be forgiven.

Just think of yourself as a projector of forgiveness, a reflector beaming out the power of forgiveness. The people that you forgive in the name and by the authority of Jesus will be forgiven. The power of that sin over their lives will be broken because you have stepped out in faith and acted as a forgiver instead of a judge, as a blesser instead of a curser.

It isn't that the people don't need to be judged, but judgment belongs to God, not to us.

God has not made us judges, He has made us forgivers. He has put into our hands something more powerful than atomic fission—the power of unilateral forgiveness. The exercise of that power makes changes for all eternity.

PART THREE:
THE RENEWED MIND IS PATIENT

THE 'LITTLE WHILES' OF LIFE
PROMISE AND PROCESS
FORGIVENESS AND DELIVERANCE

CHAPTER SIX

The 'Little Whiles' of Life

A little while, and you will see me no more; again a little while, and you will see me (John 16 : 16).

"What does He mean by 'a little while' and we will see Him no longer, and again 'a little while' and we will see Him?" the disciples wondered. After Jesus' crucifixion they were plunged into fear and despair. They lived behind locked doors for fear that the same fate which had befallen Jesus would now rise up and strike at them, who had been His followers. In their fear and despair they had forgotten the prophecy which Jesus had opened up to them: On the third day He would rise again. In their grief they had forgotten that in a little while they would see Him again. In spite of their anxiety and despair God was at work. He had a plan and a purpose which He meant to accomplish during this little while until they should see Him again.

The Watchword: God Is at Work

During this time of waiting, out of the disciples' sight, God was marvellously at work. God was defeating the principalities and powers which had kept man bound. God was laying the foundation of a salvation which would be made known to all the world. It was a time of waiting, a time of sorrow, but God was at work.

God also had a second purpose for the disciples in this time of waiting. That was to accomplish something in the lives of these disciples themselves. He wanted them, during this time, to lay hold upon the promise that they should see Him again and to live in faith—even though they weren't seeing Him. So there was a double purpose: God was working out a plan in His own sphere of activity, and He was also allowing faith and trust to grow in the hearts of the disciples.

Every Christian will experience 'little whiles' in his life, times when it seems that God almost goes away, and we have to hang on by faith until He comes again. What comes of these times of waiting depends upon how we enter into them—whether we sense the meaning and purpose of these times, or whether we just suffer through them.

Jesus sets the goal for this time of waiting when He says, "You shall know joy that no one shall take away from you." God's purpose in a time of waiting is to lead you to such a joy.

The watchword to raise up over a time of waiting is simply this: "God is at work". No other promise, no other reality can so buoy up your heart with confidence as the knowledge that God is at work. The tendency in our hearts and minds during a time of waiting is to think that God has vanished off the stage of our life. But the Bible assures us that God is at work.

What, then, is necessary if we are to live through these 'little whiles'? First of all, we need *knowledge*. We need to know that God does have a plan, and that He is accomplishing something; we are not going through a time which has no meaning. Secondly, we have to *trust*. We have to lay hold upon that knowledge and trust the Word of God. And, third, we have to exercise *persistence* in clinging to the Word of God.

Knowing the Word of God

Jesus' disciples had been given knowledge but had not really laid hold upon it. Their faith was based primarily on their first-hand experience with Jesus. Wonderful as that was, it wasn't enough to see them through that 'little while'. They needed specific knowledge from God's Word. We see this with the two disciples on the road to Emmaus, the afternoon of the Resurrection. Jesus fell in alongside them asking, "Why are you so downhearted?" They said it was because Jesus had been crucified, and "we had hoped that he was the one to deliver Israel". Then Jesus began to open up to them the Scriptures, and show them in the Word of God how it was a necessary part of God's plan that the Messiah must suffer, and through suffering enter into His glory. As He opened up to them this Word, and they gained this knowledge, their hearts burned strangely within them. They needed specific knowledge of God's plan.

In a time of trial and testing, you can't live on the memory of an experience, wonderful as it may have been. You must have specific, concrete knowledge of God's plan, promises, and purpose.

A missionary to Pakistan said, "Living out here is pretty primitive; for a Westerner it is difficult, just from a health standpoint, to live in this climate." He said that if he didn't know that God had sent him there, he couldn't stand it. That's what makes difficulty endurable: knowing without a doubt that God has put you there, and that He is working out a plan.

Scripture says that the Word of God is like a seed. A seed always has a period of growth. It is during that period of growth that you must sit and wait, so the thing that God has promised and planned for you may come to full ripeness. For He wants you to have a joy which no one can take away from you.

Think of Jesus' disciples: they had wonderful fellowship with Jesus. But Jesus had to lift their vision from that immediate friendship to the eternal fellowship which He wanted them to enjoy, a fellowship that could never be broken through all eternity. So into their life came this 'little while', during which they adjusted to God's vision of the future. Painfully they worked themselves loose from a vision which was focused upon the present time only.

God must do that with us. He may use many a 'little while' to break us loose from a short-sighted vision, to pry loose the tentacles of the present so that they no longer bind us.

God also uses these 'little whiles' of waiting to shift our focus from our own resources to His resources— from what *we* are able to do, to what *He* is able and waiting to do. In times of waiting God frustrates our own efforts to the point where we finally have to look to Him. He will let us run ourselves to the brink of exhaustion in order that He might show us His limitless resources.

One day in eternity we will look backward upon the whole period of human history, and it will be just the blink of an eye. Paul says in 2 Corinthians 4:17 that the slight afflictions of the present time are preparing for us "an eternal weight of glory". That is what is being worked out in these 'little whiles' of our lives— an eternal weight of glory beyond all comparison. We are pilgrims on this earth. We are living out a trial period during which God is preparing us for greater things.

If you know this in your mind, and believe it, you can lead a completely different life. You will move beyond wondering whether God, today or tomorrow, is going to give you this or that blessing. You will no longer live from experience to experience. You will see that there is a deeper plan, and that it includes the difficulty of these 'little whiles' in our lives.

When a 'little while' comes, it doesn't mean that you are out of contact, that God has lost all knowledge of your existence. God *does* care for you. He is at work. "They that wait upon the Lord will renew their strength. They will mount up with wings like eagles. They will run and not be weary. They will walk and not faint" (Isa. 40:31). We need that kind of knowledge; we need to know that these 'little whiles' are a specific part of God's plan for His whole church, and a specific part of His plan for our own life.

Trusting the Word of God

When you have this specific knowledge, you must lay hold upon it and trust it. You must commit yourself to God's plan.

Jesus did exactly that as He stood before Pilate. "As a lamb before its shearers is dumb, so he opened not his mouth." Jesus said nothing to defend himself. He went through the humiliation of the crucifixion because He *knew*. He had specific, concrete knowledge from Scripture that this was part of God's plan. He trusted God's Word even in the midst of the pain and humiliation.

Think of it! The Lord of creation being crucified by His own creatures. The Sinless One taking upon himself every sin ever committed by any man, woman, or child. But He *knew*—He knew that it was a part of God's plan, so He was able to endure it in silence. He was able to live through a 'little while' when God seemed to have deserted even Him, as He cried out from the Cross, "My God, my God, why hast thou forsaken me?"

The book of Revelation gives us a picture of what happened through this seemingly foolish plan of a lamb led to the slaughter. As the scroll which ushers in the happenings of the last times is about to be opened, there is sought someone to open it, but no one is found worthy. John weeps because no one is found worthy to open the scroll. As he is weeping, someone comes and touches him on the shoulder and says, "Weep not, for the Lion of the tribe of Judah is worthy to open the scroll." This is Christ—this is the Messiah! John lifts up his eyes. And does he see a lion? No, he sees one like a *lamb*, a lamb which had been slain but which is now alive. And suddenly he realizes, "The Lion is the Lamb!" The sovereign power of God was at work in the weakness of One being crucified.

Jesus trusted God's Word during that 'little while', and through that trust God brought life out of death.

Persisting in the Word of God

You must have *knowledge* to live through these 'little whiles' of life when God is working out His plans in your life. You must *trust* His Word. And then you must *persevere*.

Again, in the book of Revelation, it tells of some of the terrible calamities which will come upon the earth. It says, "This is a time for the endurance of the saints" (Rev. 13:10). This is a time to cling to God's Word even when the going gets rough.

In times when God seems distant, or when nothing seems to be happening, it's dangerously easy to fall away from God's Word, to fall into sin or despair.

Joseph was sold by his brothers as a slave and taken down into Egypt. How easy it would have been to say, "Nobody cares about me. I might as well live the way of the world, and get along as best I can." But when the wife of his master would have lured him into sin, he refused. It was a 'little while' in Joseph's life when God seemed distant. Yet he persisted in the belief that his life was still under the hand of God.

There is great temptation to fall into sin when your spiritual life is at low ebb. But you will experience ten times the spiritual growth when you cling to the Lord in a deep and dark time, as when you simply go along with the Lord in an easy time. Anybody can do that. "If you bear patiently when you are suffering *unjustly*, then you have God's approval" (1 Pet. 2:20). In these 'little whiles' God expects us to live in harmony with His will, even though we don't have the good feeling that makes it easy.

It is easy during a 'little while', to fall into despair,

to feel that God doesn't care. "Why should I go to church today? Why should I continue in my private prayers? Why should I continue in my calling? God doesn't seem to care about me any more . . ." It's easy to look out on the world and say, "There's that fellow across the street—he never gives God the time of day, and he doesn't seem to have nearly the trouble that I do." That's been said as long as people have believed in God. "The unrighteous flourish and the righteous are trampled down." It's easy to give way to despair and feel that it isn't worth it—my case isn't heard by God.

It would have been easy for Joseph to think that way when he was cast into prison. But even there he remained faithful to God. He did his little service: He helped some fellow prisoners, and God used that little service to bring him out of prison, and raise him up to a position of great authority. It was all part of God's plan of deliverance for the people of Israel. In this 'little while' of Joseph's life, this time when God seemed to have deserted him, when his own brethren had cast him off, God was at work. They meant it for evil, but God meant it for enormous good.

The 'little whiles' of our lives are not easy to endure. They aren't the days that you normally tell people about, like the days when God is close and real. But they are days when God is doing a wonderful work in your heart and life. They are days when God is working out a plan that involves you and all those with whom you will come into contact. They are the days when you take courage to raise up over your life the standard, "*Walk carefully. God is at work!*"

CHAPTER SEVEN

Promise and Process

If we are honest with ourselves, we have to admit that there is much more promised in the Bible than we have experienced. In Romans 6:14, it says, "Sin will no longer have dominion over you." Yet the experience which we have as human beings, and as Christians, is that often sin *does* catch us in its tentacles. Romans 8:8 says, "You are not in the flesh but in the spirit." Yet so often we have to confess that we are *not* in the Spirit. We are caught up in the ways of the flesh. We are addressed as "holy brethren" (Heb. 3:1), yet when we look at our own lives—and when we look at much of the history of the Christian Church—we see that it is marred by unholiness. What is a Christian to do in the face of this kind of unfulfilment? We see the promise, but experience so little of its fulfilment.

In Hebrews 3:1–6, we find an answer—simple, yet profound: "Therefore, holy brethren, who share in a heavenly call, consider Jesus, the apostle and high priest of our confession. He was faithful to him who appointed him, just as Moses also was faithful in God's house. ... And we are his house if we hold fast our confidence and pride in our hope."

What is the answer? *Consider Jesus.* Go back to the

One who started to build this house (see 1 Peter 2:5). Go back to Jesus. Ask quite soberly "Is He able to finish what He began? Is Jesus able to complete this house which He has started to build?" And the answer is, "Yes, He is finishing the house. He is finishing it on schedule."

Now if this is true, if Jesus is going to get His house built, why do we find our Christian lives (which is His house) oftentimes plagued with uncertainty, doubt, and frustration? Much of this can be traced to the fact that whereas we have embraced the *promises* of God with our faith and with our understanding, we have failed to grasp the *process* by which He brings these promises to fulfilment. The Bible not only tells us about the promises. It also details the process by which the promises come to pass.

When I was four or five years old, I used to climb up on my dad's lap and ask him to read me the comic strips. If he didn't have time, I'd badger my older brother into doing it.

"I'll be glad when you get into school," my brother would sigh. "Then you can read the comic strips yourself."

That became the goal of my five-year-old life: When I got into school, I'd be able to read the comic strips by myself!

When my first day of school finally arrived, I was all dressed and ready—sitting out on the front steps at 5.30 in the morning. At last the hour came, and I trooped off to school. Our class went through the routine of the first day, having seats assigned and getting acquainted. At the sound of the last bell I streaked for home, came tearing into the house, threw open the evening paper, and flopped down to look at the comic strips. And then I burst out crying. I couldn't read!

My hopes were so fixed on the *promise* that I had failed to grasp the *process* by which that promise would come into fulfilment. It was perfectly true as my brother had said that when I went to school, I could read the comic strips. But there was a process, a time gap, during which I would move into the fulfilment of that promise.

God's Time

God's plans always involve a process which moves in a period of time, God's time. The Bible explains God's time this way: "With the Lord one day is as a thousands years, and a thousand years as one day" (2 Pet. 3:8). This means that time is relative for God. It can be either shorter or longer than our time, depending upon God's purposes. Time to Him is like a rubber band. He can stretch it out or He can compress it.

When we talk about a process, we have to recognize that the time factor is according to God's time, not ours. That may cause frustration if we haven't beheld Jesus long enough to get the feeling of His time in a given situation.

God will stretch out time as He has done, for instance, in regard to the setting up of His kingdom. Anyone with a fraction of God's power could have set up a world government in a matter of years. In our own lifetime, we have seen men and nations come close to world domination in a few years' time. But God has taken 2000 years, and the kingdom still has not been established. But if we reckon by the word in 2

Peter, it has been only two days according to God's time.

On the other hand, God can compress time. Normally water falls upon a vineyard as rain, goes through a process of being taken up into a vine, grapes are produced, and finally, after more time elapses, the water is converted into wine. On one occasion Jesus changed water into wine instantaneously. Usually, if a person has a fever, he rests in bed, and in time the fever will pass. Peter's mother-in-law had a fever. Jesus took her by the hand, and she was healed of the fever instantly. God can compress time or He can stretch it out.

God's Materials

God is in the process of building a building. It's a house of living stones (1 Pet. 2:5). We are the stones. What does this process of building a building involve? First of all, the materials must be gathered. That suggests the outreach of the Church to bring in those who have not yet become Christians, who have not yet heard the message. That's evangelism—gathering together the living stones. At this stage of the process, there is great concentration upon the individual. It's my salvation which is at the centre of focus; it's my Saviour, Jesus, who comes to my awareness. This phase of the building programme is filled with great joy for the 'stones'. We suddenly find out what our life is all about. We find a new centre for our life, Jesus.

Shaping the Materials

But that isn't the end of the process. It's only the beginning. Now comes the business of shaping the materials, and then of storing them, perhaps, and waiting until an actual phase of the building gets underway. This is what we call the process of sanctification, or Christian growth.

This process may be somewhat less exciting, and is usually less comfortable, than the process of being taken in. Now the stone masons come up and begin to chip away at the stones, to get them shaped and ready to be fitted into their particular part of the building. When the Holy Spirit begins to chip away at you, knock off this rough edge, round off that corner, it is not always a comfortable process.

Then comes the time when He sets you over on a pile, and you just wait, because another phase of the building operation is being taken care of. You know what it's like on a building site. Over there you see big stacks of timber sitting. Over here a pile of stone waiting. Nothing is happening. This is one of the hardest things to endure. It's here that many Christians fall away. They tumble off the building site down into the ravine and get lost because they can't stand the boredom.

There is a piling up and waiting process that is a part of Christian growth. Nothing happens. You can't understand why. "Where is all the old joy? Where is that closeness to Jesus that I once knew?" He's just as close to you as ever He was. You're just as much a part of His plan as ever you were. But the process has moved into a new phase. It's in a waiting phase.

Picture a tree that drops its leaves in the autumn. It seems bare and lifeless. It goes into a period of dormancy. But what is that period of dormancy preparing for? What lies ahead? New life, new fruitfulness! In California, after Christmas, we prune our poinsettias and they become bare, ugly stumps. Sometimes you feel like a bare, ugly stump. You feel there is nothing happening in your Christian life. But that isn't true. God's process is moving ahead on schedule.

Consider Jesus

The Bible says, "Look to Jesus". Don't look at that stump that you think your life is right now. Forget that. Look to Jesus. Look to Jesus until He puts back into your heart and understanding a vision of His building programme, until He filters into your thought the conviction and assurance that He's going to finish His building on schedule.

It is well to look carefully at our own lives from time to time, because it's possible that we've rolled off the building site. It is well to see if we are still in the fellowship of believers, if we are still having our times of prayer. But if these things are in order, if we are genuinely seeking God, yet don't feel close to Him, then the Bible says, "Consider Jesus". He is going to finish the job that He has begun. He has started a wonderful programme. If you look to Him, He is going to put back into your heart the conviction that He is doing the job. He is involved in this process of building.

When you are very close to it, sometimes you can't see the shape of a construction project. There is a man who has been at work for twenty years, carving the world's largest sculpture out of the raw face of a mountain. On completion it will be a sculpture of the Indian chief, Crazy Horse. The tools involved in shaping this largest sculpture ever attempted by man are a bulldozer and dynamite blasts—moving the whole side of the mountain, hundreds of tons of stone. When you're up close, watching him and his bulldozer, you can't see anything but the raw side of a mountain and a man pushing heaps of stones around. He himself, at that point, can't really see what it is going to look like. But he has the vision in his mind. He knows where the stones have to be moved. When you back off, you do begin to see, roughly, the outline of what he is making out of that huge mountain.

When you're up close to your own experience, oftentimes you get a distorted view of the finished product. That's why the Bible says, "Consider Jesus". Get into fellowship with Him so you can get His perspective from heaven, looking down. Read the book of Ephesians and catch the picture, the blueprint, of the Church. Recognize that you're one little stone in the midst of it, and God is going to finish the job. He's going to finish it on schedule.

This is one of the most encouraging words in Scripture for times when nothing seems to be happening, or times when things seem even to go against our Christian faith—when people say, "What's your belief, what's your faith, what have you got to show for it?" And often the answer is, "We can't show anything for it." All we can do is *consider Jesus* until that hope becomes a living reality in our hearts.

A person says, "Why do you believe in Christianity? Two thousand years have gone. Where is the promise of His coming?" Yes, two thousand years have gone. But God is right on schedule. He's building His kingdom. With the Psalmist, we can laugh at the plotting and planning of kings and nations, because we know that God is building His kingdom.

We know from human experience that when a foundation is laid, a building will rise on that site. And, by faith in God's Word, we know that the foundation has been laid for a building not made with hands, eternal in the heavens, the New Jerusalem. God is in the process of building it now. He has called us to be living stones in that building. Don't get discouraged when times of inactivity come along. Don't roll off the building site. Don't let times of silence and quietness and boredom get to you, because *He is going to finish the job!*

Often when you get involved in a building programme, there are frustrating delays and roadblocks. Sometimes it looks like semi-organized confusion on the building site. But the work goes on. The workmen show up at their appointed time. Finally, the building is finished. The process is completed. The promise of the original plan is fulfilled. And those who have persevered to the end are on hand to share the glory of the dedication.

CHAPTER EIGHT

Forgiveness and Deliverance

"Lord, I did it again. I *did it again*!" How often do we have to say those words? How often do we have to return to the Lord with the same old sin, the same old failure, the same old hang-up? We confess it and we are forgiven, but somehow or other we are not delivered. We are not changed. We are not renewed. Intuitively we know that there should be progress in the Christian life. We want to see a growth in Godlike living. Yet so often the very thing we strive for does not become a part of our experience. Why? The answer hinges on a seldom-recognized distinction between forgiveness and deliverance.

In Isaiah 51:5, the Lord says: "My deliverance draws near speedily, my salvation has gone forth." *But it hasn't yet arrived.* Forgiveness is like a rocket which has been launched from heaven towards you; the forgiveness is granted from the moment of launching. But deliverance does not come until that rocket arrives here on earth. The experience of many is that their rocket is hung up in mid-air somewhere: Forgiveness has been granted, but deliverance has not arrived.

The whole world watched on television when the Apollo Mission made its first excursion to the moon.

We were gripped by it from the moment it blasted off until the dramatic moment of splashdown. We wouldn't have been satisfied—indeed, it would have been tragic —if that last phase of splashdown had not been completed successfully. The 51st Psalm describes a divine mission of forgiveness and deliverance, from its beginning in the mind of God, till its splashdown in the heart and experience of man.

Conviction from Heaven

The first operation is this: God sends a triggering impulse down to earth—He convicts of sin. Psalm 51 was written by David after he had sinned against the Lord by committing adultery with Bathsheba and engineering the murder of her husband. The prophet Nathan came to him and told him the story of a man who had one lamb which he loved so much that he brought it into the house with him, raising it like one of his own children. Then he told of a wealthy man who had many flocks and herds. When someone came to visit this wealthy man, instead of taking a sheep out of his own flock, he went and took the lamb from the man who had only one. What should be done with such a man? David's quick reply was, "Such a man should be put to death!" He saw immediately the injustice of it. Then Nathan said, "You are the man. You have many wives and riches, and yet you took away the wife of this man who had just one wife whom he loved dearly. *You are the man.*"

That's the triggering impulse from heaven down to earth. That impulse convicts us of those things in our lives that are not pleasing to the Lord. We may have considered these things relatively harmless, but the Lord takes sin far more seriously than we do. Why? Because He loves us so much. He knows that "without holiness no one will see the Lord" (Heb. 12:14). He knows that repentance and forgiveness is the key to heaven, and there is no other.

We have to say, "Lord, show me my sin." We have to want to be exposed—not run and hide—but want to be exposed. "Lord, I want to know what in my life is not pleasing to you." Then we have to be ready to have that answer come to us. That means that our ear must be open to our brethren, for they oftentimes see our sin more clearly than we do.

David had blinded himself to his sin because he didn't want to face up to it. But Nathan saw it. That's the way we are by nature. We need to pray, "Cleanse thou me of hidden faults (Ps. 19:12). Send me a Nathan, if I need such a jolt to bring it to my attention."

Oh, to have our ears opened to others—yes, to our wives, to our husbands, even to our children, and children to their parents—that we might be cleansed of those things which are displeasing to the Lord, those things that He knows are keeping our lives from becoming what He wants them to be. For it says in the 90th Psalm, "Thou hast set our iniquities before thee, our secret sins in the light of thy countenance." God sees these things and He sees us, and therefore He sends this triggering impulse down to earth to convict us, to bring us to account for those things in our lives which are not right.

Confession from Earth

The second step is that we send a triggering response back to heaven. We confess our sins and ask forgiveness. We must agree with God in His judgment; His triggering impulse must find an answering response in us. That's what it means to confess our sin: to agree with the blameless judgment of God.

When his sin was exposed, David responded, "I have sinned against the Lord." He sent his answering response back to heaven.

What is the result of the triggering response that goes from earth back to heaven? The result is forgiveness, immediate forgiveness. Jesus, in Luke 18:9–14, tells the story of two men who went into the temple to pray—a publican, that is, a man who was looked down on in society, a man who was segregated from polite society; and a Pharisee, who was the quintessence of morality and fine society. These two men prayed, each in his own way. The publican prayed for mercy. He sent that triggering response back to God and said, "Lord, be merciful to me a sinner." Jesus said, "That man went down to his house justified." *As soon as he spoke, the forgiveness was granted*. God beamed forgiveness towards the publican's heart immediately— just as the astronauts, when they were on the moon, could beam their voices back down to earth instantly.

Deliverance Is Launched

Too often we stop here. "I'm forgiven. Sometime, in heaven, I'll be perfected. Sometime, in heaven, I'll be cleansed of these things that are constantly tripping me up." But this is where we need to lay hold upon God for the conclusion to this mission. Boldly we must declare, "Lord, I'm not going to give up on this mission until splashdown. I'm not content with just forgiveness, for You say that You will *cleanse me* of all unrighteousness."

1 John 1:9 says, "If we confess our sins, he is faithful and just and will *forgive* our sins . . ." But the verse doesn't end there. It goes on and says, ". . . *and cleanse us from all unrighteousness.*" That is deliverance.

So, now, there has been the triggering impulse from heaven to convict us of our sin. There has been the triggering response from earth asking for forgiveness. And, on the basis of that, God launches His rocket of deliverance.

Faith Fuels the Rocket of Deliverance

God delivers and cleanses us through faith. "He delivered us from so deadly a peril . . . on him we have set our hope that he will deliver us again" (2 Cor. 1:10). We must believe and act upon what God has done, and therefore what must surely come to pass. The rocket of deliverance which God launches from heaven is fuelled by faith, and many a deliverance, many an answer to prayer, is simply hung up in mid-air. It ran out of fuel. There was not the exercise of faith to bring it down to earth.

Think of Abraham, as he is described in the fourth chapter of Romans. God had launched a rocket aimed directly at him, the promise that he should have a son. That promise was a long time in arriving. The rocket had a long journey to travel. But the Bible says, "No distrust made Abraham waver concerning the promise of God, but he grew strong in faith." He fuelled that rocket with faith, as he gave glory to God, fully convinced that God would do what He had promised. That was why his faith was reckoned to him as righteousness. He knew that the rocket which had been launched was going to arrive.

We might have had some uneasy moments when we heard that the astronauts were lifting off from the moon's surface. But there were not many who really doubted that they would return safely. We believed. We waited. We trusted. We watched. And . . . they arrived.

Faith Overcomes Satanic Roadblocks

Faith is a battle. Satan roadblocks the rocket. There are spiritual meteorites out there, aimed to destroy your rocket before it ever arrives.

In the tenth chapter of Daniel, we see Daniel in Babylon confessing his sins and the sins of his people. He was sending off this triggering response to heaven. It was twenty-one days before God's rocket arrived. And when it arrived, the angel who was the messenger said, "From the moment your prayer went forth the answer was sent." The rocket had been launched immediately, but "the prince of the power of Persia withstood me for twenty-one days". That rocket of answered prayer was getting spiritual opposition as it sped towards its destination. But Daniel kept believing, and the archangel Michael was sent to deliver it from the power of the Prince of Persia, that is, from the evil spiritual power that dominated that area. Only then did the answer come through. Faith is a battle!

God Selects the Landing Site

Faith is open. It is open to receive the rocket at any splashdown point that God designates. Often we may miss the answer because we are waiting at Landing Area Number Two when God has charted it to come in on Number Ten. Psalm 51 mentions different landing areas, different ways that the Lord delivers us from the power of sin. "Teach me wisdom in my secret heart" is one area. You can have wisdom in the head, but when wisdom gets into the secret heart, it's something that assures you, "Ah, now I'm in tune. Now I'm right with God."

"Purge me" and "wash me" are other landing areas. Ephesians 5:26 says that Jesus cleanses us with the washing of the Word. This is another way in which deliverance comes.

At another landing area it says, "Create in me a clean heart, O God"—a clean heart, a heart with new affection, a heart with new loyalty. You begin to like new things. You begin to appreciate new kinds of people.

Jim Brown, a Presbyterian minister in Pennsylvania, once said, "The one thing that used to irk me more than anything else was people who would come up and ask me, 'Are you saved?' I know now why it irked me. I wasn't saved!" He continued, "I was a Christian Socialist. I wouldn't call myself a Christian. When they laid the cornerstone of the United Nations Building in New York, I thought the millennium was right around the corner. But then the Lord found me—and now the Lord's people are the ones I enjoy being with." He received a new heart, new relationships, new affections.

The Lord delivered him from bondages of the past.

Splashdown: A Changed Life

What's the conclusion of all this? When we lay hold upon God and say, "I will not cease to pray and believe until that rocket arrives, until I am delivered of these things that are tripping me up ... *then I will teach transgressors thy ways.*" Then I will have a testimony that rings true, because it is rooted in reality. It's a changed life that makes people sit up and take notice.

And how does this change come about? The rocket arrives, *bearing Jesus into our lives.* He is the life-changer. He is the one we must pray for. "Lord, I will not quit praying and believing You until Jesus comes in to make this very change that has caused You grief and that I've had to confess before You now. Until I am changed in that area of my life I will not cease to believe You and trust You. Though I have to wait, and pray long, and the battle is difficult, I will believe."

Jesus is the life-changer. It was after Jesus went into the house of Zacchaeus that Zacchaeus could say, "Lord, if I have cheated any man, I will restore four-fold." What made the change? *Jesus had come into his house.* Jesus is the rocket—the rocket that God has sent for your deliverance.

Don't rest until splashdown. Don't be content until deliverance comes. God knows how long it is going to take. He knows the barriers that need to be overcome. But He promises in His Word that He will cleanse us from *all* unrighteousness, make us new people through the indwelling of His Holy Spirit.

PART FOUR: THE RENEWED MIND ACCEPTS DISCIPLINE

THE TOOL OF TROUBLE
THE FIRE, LORD, NOT THE JUNK HEAP!

CHAPTER NINE

The Tool of Trouble

What is the essential difference between the life of someone who is a Christian and someone who is not a Christian? A non-Christian is independent of Jesus Christ. A Christian is dependent on Jesus Christ in every aspect of his life. The whole process of Christian growth boils down to this: *Learning to depend on Jesus in every circumstance*.

God uses many ways to teach us to become dependent on Jesus Christ: instruction, preaching, example. Teaching, however, can become stalled at the level of theory or potential. Often the teaching alone is not enough to convince us deep down inside that we need to depend on Jesus Christ in every circumstance of life. Deep within us, beneath the level that can be reached by our conscious will, exist little pockets of independence which insist that we can live out this or that aspect of our lives on our own. The Holy Spirit wants to reach down into the depths of our being and teach us, not merely in words or in theory, but in reality, to depend on Jesus in every circumstance.

In order to do this, the Holy Spirit brings into action a very special tool called Trouble. This is a tool which God has designed to get down into the depths of our being. It is designed to fulfil a twofold function: it has a *cutting edge* and an *etching point*. The cutting edge of trouble exposes our weakness. The etching point inscribes upon the picture of God's strength. Trouble exposes our weakness so that we can learn to draw upon God's strength. That is the particular job the tool of trouble does for each of us as it is used by the Holy Spirit.

The Cutting Edge of Trouble

First of all, the Holy Spirit uses trouble to *expose our weakness*. This weakness falls into two basic categories: The weakness of our *circumstances*—those things *outside* of us we depend on; and the weakness of our *character*—those things *inside* of us we depend on.

The Weakness of Our Circumstances

The cutting edge of trouble exposes the weakness of our circumstances. Economic circumstances, for instance, can wield great influence upon our lives. The Bible illustrates this in the parable of the Rich Fool.

In your own life, without any warning, you can have hundreds of pounds of unexpected expenses; inflation can eat into your savings. You discover just how dependent you are on material things. The Holy Spirit may use economic trouble to expose those things in our lives which are not essentially related to Jesus.

Calamities come to show the weakness of our social environment—from a little thing like a traffic jam, to a major thing like war. Overnight a stable situation can crumble. God allows it to happen. He allows the cutting edge of trouble to knife into our undue dependency upon our surroundings.

We may think that we have stable relationships in regard to our standing with other people. But God will cut into that with the sharp edge of trouble. Jesus himself found this aspect of His life put to the test. He came into Jerusalem on Palm Sunday. The crowd shouted, "Hosanna to the Son of David!" Five days later the crowd's enthusiasm evaporated. God put it to the test. If Jesus had been depending on the support of the crowd, He would have been thoroughly discouraged. The first thing that trouble does is to show us how helpless and needy we really are.

The Weakness of Our Character

God also wants us to recognize the weaknesses in our own character. We tend to depend upon certain characteristics within ourselves to bring us through difficult situations.

Jesus warned His disciples that there was going to be a falling away. Peter said, "Not me, Lord. Maybe the rest, but not good old solid rock-like Peter! Though everybody else desert you, I won't desert you, Lord." Jesus shook His head and said, "Oh, Peter, Satan has demanded to have you. You've put yourself out on a limb. God has no alternative but to take the knife of trouble and expose the weakness of your vaunted courage."

The Holy Spirit put Peter into the crucible of trouble —into "Satan's sifter". There he discovered that he did not have the courage to stand up for Jesus. Jesus knew what was in Peter's character, but it took trouble to expose that weakness so that *Peter* knew it. That's what trouble does. It brings us to an awareness of something that God knew all along.

In our relationships with other people we have to learn not to depend on the merits of our own character. Have you been disappointed or even shocked by the impatience, the hatred, the resentment that suddenly bursts out of you under extreme testing in a situation? You say, "Oh! I didn't know that was in me!" But God knew it was in you. So He took the sharp knife of trouble and exposed that weakness, so that you could recognize your need for a strength beyond yourself.

Sören Kierkegaard, the 19th-century Danish theologian and philosopher, tells a story that marked him all his life. He saw a man whose relationship with God apparently stood in good order. And yet, when his young son died, this man stood by the graveside and shook his fist towards heaven crying, "Is this the way You treat me after all I've done for You?" Suddenly the weakness of his character stood nakedly exposed. His relationship to God was not a relationship of love and trust, but one of duty and keeping the rules, and being paid for what you do. Not the mentality of a son, but of a slave. The sharp knife of trouble exposed his weakness.

Perhaps you are in the midst of trouble even as you read this. What does God want you to do when you come into trouble? Trouble knifes you open and you see the weakness in your life. The things outside you collapse. The things inside you crumble. What are you to do? That's where the second function of the tool of trouble comes into play.

The Etching Point of Trouble

On this raw, exposed part of our life, God begins to etch a picture and a promise of the strength and the resources of God. Consider two questions at this point: When the Holy Spirit wields His tool of trouble upon your life, does it make you *bitter* or does it make you *better*? Do you cry out for *deliverance* or for *development*?

Trouble Can Make You Bitter

The words "bitter" and "better" are very similar. Just one letter makes the difference: the *I*. And that is the key. If you focus upon the *I* in your situation of trouble, you will become bitter and hard. If you look at your own misery and begin to wallow around in self-pity, bitterness will overcome you.

Let's not kid ourselves about trouble. There's nothing magic about it. Trouble is morally neutral. Trouble makes some people bitter, hard, and resentful against life and people. It all depends upon the way you respond to it. If you focus upon the *I*, the ego, what is happening to *me* in this situation, then it will make you bitter. Or, if you look at your own resources ("Now what can *I* do to get out of this?"), summon up all of your strength, and work out some kind of solution that will bring you through after a fashion—again, it will tend to make you hard. You become convinced that you have to raise up even higher barriers against calamity.

Trouble Can Make You Better

If you focus not upon the *I*, but upon God, then an experience of trouble can make you infinitely better. That's what happened to St. Paul. Look at the troubles which he lists in 2 Corinthians 11:19–12:10. But he received all of them *as from the hand of the Lord*. His focus in time of trouble was upon God.

"Unto *You*, O Lord, do I look in my time of distress. This trouble has come upon me, Lord, but I am looking to You." I look at the Cross, and ask, "Lord, what is it in me that requires this kind of discipline and training? What is it in my character, or my depending upon circumstances, that requires such rough handling?" Such honest searching can issue in life-renewing repentance.

But we do not stop at the Cross. We look also to the open heaven, saying, "Lord, what resources of Yours do You want to bring into this situation to redeem it, to change it? What aspect of Christ's character can come into me now? What of His patience and love and understanding can begin to recharge my whole inner being with something from beyond myself?"

As you look to God, the heavens open up. God begins to show you how you can draw upon the resources of heaven to fill up this emptiness and weakness that has been exposed in your own life. God never exposes weakness to shame us, to make us feel helpless and frightened. He only wants to tell us, "I never meant for you to live a life independent of Me. I created you a dependent being. If you are not depending on Me, you are going to be depending upon some false god." The human creature was created for dependency —utter, complete dependency. When God exposes our weakness, it is only to bring us back to bed-rock, so that we can build our life on the right foundation.

Deliverance or Development

When the Holy Spirit wields the tool of trouble upon your life, do you look for deliverance, or do you look for development? If you continually and habitually refuse to meet trouble head-on, you miss the Holy Spirit's purpose. You've been cut open, your weakness is exposed, but then you tuck yourself together and dodge away from the trouble. All you've had is a painful experience and nothing has been gained by it.

This is our human tendency. We cry out, "Lord, deliver me! What can I do to get out of this situation?" If we listen, the voice of God will say, "I don't intend for you to get out of it. I intend for you to go *through* it. The purpose for which this trouble has come is not that you be delivered, but that you be developed—that you become more like Jesus as you go through this experience."

Every obstacle in our path becomes an occasion for us to ponder, "What is it in me that must be brought to zero, and what is it in Christ that will flood into that vacuum and fill it up with the strength and power of heaven?" As you look at the situation, you discover the unsearchable wisdom of God in planning the kind of things that come into your life. They are absolutely designed to bring forth in you something of Christ— to expose a weakness, so that Christ can fill it with His strength.

The Holy Spirit is a master-craftsman in fashioning us after the likeness of Christ. He uses many different methods, many tools. Trouble is one of His tools, a precious tool. As you look at the pattern of your own life, and you see trouble staring you in the face, consider that God has sent it for a very special purpose: to expose your weakness, so that you can learn to draw on the strength of Christ.

CHAPTER TEN

The Fire, Lord, Not the Junk Heap!

An American television personality, Arthur Godfrey, likes to tell the story of his acquaintance with an old blacksmith. He used to watch this man at his work, as he took each piece of metal in his experienced hand to examine it. Some he would throw on to one pile, to be worked on later. But others he would glance at and throw on to the junk heap.

Godfrey asked, "Why is it that you throw some on to the junk heap and some over here?"

The blacksmith said, "I can see that some of that metal will be useful when it is put through the fire. There is something in it that will let it go through the fire and come out refined and perfected. But the other metal is useless—it cannot take the fire, so I have to toss it over on to the junk heap."

That experience made a lasting impression on Godfrey. It became symbolic of some of the experiences he had later in life. He recognized that many of the difficult experiences he had to go through were the very things that tested and proved him, and made him a better man. It became something of a motto in his life. When he faced one of these difficult situations, he would say, "Lord, the fire, not the junk heap!"

What could be so tragic as to be set aside and declared, "No longer useful to the Lord"? How much better to go through the fires of testing and proving, if in the end you come out refined and purified and able to be used once again by God—and used in a more expansive way than you had been used before. For this is a spiritual truth : the law of testing and proving, the law of the fire, equips us for the Lord's service.

A scientist doesn't sit back and complain about God's laws, nor try to disregard them. He learns what they are and then he adapts his experiments accordingly. The great team of scientists which put a man on the moon would never have done it if they had rebelled against the laws of physics and chemistry by which they were able to accomplish that feat. They had to learn these laws, and then put them to use. There are laws for spiritual living which are just as valid and just as pervasive as the laws of physics and chemistry.

A brickmaker knows that before he can build a house of brick, the bricks have to go through fire. And the Lord knows that before He can build a spiritual house, His building stones, which are human lives, have to go through the fire.

In Luke 12:49–52, Jesus speaks about this refining process under three figures: *fire*, *baptism*, and *division*—"I came to cast *fire* upon the earth; and would that it were already kindled! I have a *baptism* to be baptized with; and how I am constrained until it is accomplished! Do you think that I have come to give peace on earth? No, I tell you, but rather *division*; for henceforth in one house there will be five divided, three against two and two against three."

Fire

Fire in the Bible does three things. First of all, it *judges*. Jeremiah 4:4 says that the word of the Lord will come out and judge the people and cause them to repent, "lest my wrath go forth like fire, and burn with none to quench it, because of the evil of your doings".

Fire symbolizes God's holy wrath coming down upon the affairs of men and judging them. This kind of preaching has fallen on unpopular days. We don't like to hear about the stern judge, and yet that's the God we read about in the Bible. The God of love is also a God of judgment. He hates sin with a holy passion, so He comes with fires of judgment.

Secondly, fire *refines*. Zechariah 13:9 says, "And I will put this third into the fire, and refine them as one refines silver, and test them as gold is tested." And Malachi 3:2-3, "For he is like a refiner's fire and like fullers' soap; he will sit as a refiner and purifier of silver, and he will purify the sons of Levi and refine them like gold and silver." We know what a fire does when it purifies a metal. It takes away all foreign substances. Only the pure metal comes out. That's what God's judgment does—it removes our impurities, it reduces us to just that person whom God can use.

Then, finally, fire *transforms*. This is the symbol which we get in Leviticus where the offering is laid upon the altar and is burned up. And what happens? It becomes smoke which rises and becomes a *pleasing odour* to the Lord. It is transformed from flesh into smoke. This is a symbol of a transformed life. Fire does all these things.

Looking at His life ahead, as He headed toward the

Cross, Jesus said, "I came to cast fire upon the earth, and would that it were already kindled!" He longed for this process to get under way because this was necessary in order for His work to be fully accomplished.

Jesus still looks forward to the fulfilment of this. Where will it begin? Not 'out there' in the world. The work of cleansing and transformation must begin in the household of God. The impurities in the world grieve God. But the impurities in the Church grieve God even more.

The Church is supposed to be that wellspring of purity which will help purify the world. If that well is polluted, then God's plan and God's kingdom are in low estate. So He says, "Judgment must begin at the household of God" (1 Pet. 4 : 17).

That was Jesus' meaning when He came into Jerusalem, cleansed the Temple, and threw out all the moneychangers. Why? Because if this house was not right, if this house was not functioning with honesty and integrity, what could ever be expected of those outside? Until there is judgment in the Church, we should not expect judgments to fall on the world.

Sometimes Christians take an almost unhealthy pleasure in speaking about the judgments of God upon the world—like John and James, when a town in Samaria wouldn't accept Jesus. They said, "Lord, shall we call fire down from heaven, like Elijah, and destroy them?" But Jesus said, "You don't know what Spirit you are of. You don't know that before that happens, *you* are going to experience the fire. You yourself will first go through the judgment."

Can we say, as Jesus did, "Oh, that the fires of God

were already at work in my own life—that the fires of judgment and refining and transformation were already taking their effect upon me"? Until that happens, nothing of lasting worth can come out of our lives.

While Paul was still a young man, he was a member of the high court of Judaism, the Sanhedrin. He was advancing beyond all of his age, so zealous was he for the tradition of his fathers. And then he met Jesus. His whole life was transformed. All of these things were submitted to the fire of judgment, refining, and purifying. The dross was purged away, and he could say, "I count everything as loss because of the surpassing worth of knowing Christ Jesus my Lord" (Phil. 3:8).

Some have had God's fire kindled in their lives. They have come to a new awareness of His power and reality, and this has not been altogether accepted by members of their own families, by friends, by associates. The whole set of personal relationships has gone through the refining fires. Could you say, in such a test, "Lord, the fire, not the junk heap"? What if it means that I must restructure my friendships? Perhaps I must accept from those very close to me rebuke or disdain. It may take that kind of refining before I can become useful for Him.

Spiritual junk heaps are littered with the lives of those who would not accept the disapproval of other people, who scorned or disdained their faith. "No longer useful to the Lord"—a terrible banner to be draped over one's life.

Are you ready to face this also in regard to your *church*? "Lord, the fire, not the junk heap!" Would you be ready to accept the fact that your church was not going to be simply a comfortable, respectable place—that you and your church may have to go through the fires of reproach and criticism, to come to that place of naked willingness to obey God, no matter what? Only the church that is tested by fire is going to be useful to God.

Baptism

"I have a baptism to be baptized with; and how I am constrained [how I am boxed in] until it is accomplished!" Baptism in the Bible is a symbol of death and resurrection. There are at least four baptisms mentioned in the New Testament.

There is the baptism with water, first of all, where you are separated from Satan, sin, and death. They are "drowned out" in the waters of baptism (see 1 Cor. 10 : 1–2), and you are raised to a new life with God.

There is the baptism with the Holy Spirit. Here is where all of your power and effectiveness go to the death. Then you rise to power in Christ, by the Holy Spirit. You find a new source of power in Him—a death and resurrection.

The third type of baptism is baptism with fire. That's when many of the old things in your life are purged away, so the new life in Christ can grow.

Then, finally, in Luke 12 : 50, Jesus speaks of the baptism of suffering and death; we can also call it a "baptism of blood". "I have a baptism to be baptized with" —and His eyes were looking straight towards the Cross. This baptism is the death of my own productivity. My own life now can produce nothing. Jesus said, "Unless a grain of wheat fall into the ground and

die, it remains alone; but if it dies it bears much fruit."
Death and resurrection. Jesus looked at this baptism of
suffering, this baptism of going all the way to serve and
suffer for others, and He said, "Oh, how I am straight-
ened, how I am held in, until it be accomplished!"

Our effectiveness is limited until we have this baptism of suffering and death. Until our lives become
nothing, there can be no fruit. It doesn't make sense to
human reasoning. But it is God's way. Can we say with
Jesus, "Oh, how I am constrained until my own life
becomes nothing, in order that God's life can begin to
grow up in me and begin to function through me"?

Are we ready in our own personal lives to die to
privileges, to comforts, to personal interests, in order
that someone else might get the life of God in him?
Paul says in 2 Corinthians 4:4, "Death is at work in us,
but life in you." As we die to our own personal interests and privileges, that opens the doorway for life to
spring up in somebody else.

Evan Roberts, the great leader of the Welsh revival
in 1905–1906, was called by God to be the main
spokesman of that revival. When he realized that God
had chosen him, he went out into the field and wept all
night, because he knew it was a sentence of death. He
knew that from then on his time was not his own, his
comforts and privileges would be sacrificed. His whole
life would have to be surrendered for that revival. But
oh! the life that came forth from that revival, and is
still at work in the Church today, because a man was
willing to take his baptism of death.

Years later, Evan Roberts was asked, "Will we ever
see another revival like the Welsh revival?" He answered, "Who is willing to pay the price?"

That's what Jesus meant when He said, "If any man would come after me, let him deny himself and take up his cross and follow me." It means to follow Him in giving up our privileges, our time, our own pet pleasures, in order that somebody else might come to life.

No real life is going to spring forth from a Christian fellowship until that kind of a death is accepted. Even a small fellowship could shake the world, if its members were ready to die to their own privileges; if each individual would say, "My time is no longer my own, my money is no longer my own, my privileges are no longer my own, my family is no longer my own. I am in the hands of God just as surely as Jesus was when He went to the Cross." That kind of fellowship would shake the world.

Division

Lastly, Jesus speaks of division. He said, "I did not come to bring peace upon the earth, but division." Division is a basic principle of God's dealing with men. He separates people in order to use them. This, again, is a painful proposition. He took Abraham away from his family in Ur of the Chaldees, saying, "Go into the land that I will show you and be a separate people." He took Israel out of all the nations of the earth and said, "Be a separate people. Don't mix with the heathen around you; be a holy people, set aside for my purposes."

He says today to the Christian Church, "You are a peculiar people. Keep yourself unspotted from the world. Be a separate people." That means purging. It means going through fire to become separate, distinct, looked upon as something different, even peculiar. If we are unwilling to be different, we can't be useful to God.

"Lord, the fire, not the junk heap! Rather the fires that divide, separate, and put me in a place where You alone have access to me than to go along and be a nice, friendly person in the world where anybody has access to my time, anybody has access to my opinions and ideas, but I'm no longer useful to You."

What does division do? Division, when it comes about because of Jesus, *keeps us close to Him*. Only by separation from indifferent and ungodly influences can you keep close to Jesus. Don't fall into the trap of thinking that you are a great tower of strength, can mix with the world indiscriminately, and still stay close to Jesus.

This does not mean to take yourself out of the world. But it does mean that you never become a part of the world—a part of its system, its thinking, its way of acting, its way of believing. And it means that you must spend a generous part of your time in the company of other Christians, because you cannot abide alone.

People have mentioned this in regard to vacations, for instance. One goes on vacation and is cut off from other Christians. For a month one experiences only minimal Christian influence. The result? One comes back physically rested, perhaps, but spiritually depleted. One might have been with very good friends of bygone days, but still the spirit has been depleted, because the principle of separation is a basic spiritual law: You must first be strengthened by one another; then you are able to go out and share your faith. If you do not have a place where you can be a separate people, where you can be strengthened and built up, your faith will be dissipated.

Jesus never promised that the life of a disciple would be easy. He said, "In this world you will have persecution; in this world you will have the fire, the baptism of suffering, and division." But He said, "Be of good cheer. I have overcome the world."

This is the joy that Christians share. They are a company of people who are being prepared for His return. They are a company of people who are being prepared for the kingdom that Jesus is going to establish. He cannot establish it with pieces from the junk heap. He will only establish it with human lives, with fellowships, that have come through the fire. When the dross and the impurities have floated away, He will take these lives, tested and proved through suffering and judgment, and with them He will build His kingdom.

Lord, the fire, not the junk heap!

PART FIVE: THE RENEWED MIND PRAYS WITH CONFIDENCE

FIVE KEYS TO ANSWERED PRAYER
PRAYING IN THE NAME OF JESUS

CHAPTER ELEVEN

Five Keys to Answered Prayer

What percentage of your prayers get answered? One per cent? Two? Five? Ten?

Some people say, "God always answers prayer: Sometimes 'Yes', sometimes 'No', sometimes 'Wait'." There is truth in this, and a No or a Wait answer can teach us much as Christians—things like surrender and patience.

But most of us, when we talk about answers to prayer, mean Yes answers. That's the commonsense meaning, and it's the meaning the Bible normally uses. "All the promises of God find their Yes in Christ" (2 Cor. 1:20).

When Jesus encouraged His disciples to pray with persistence. He meant to pray for a Yes answer. When the Apostle Paul urged the congregations in Philippi, Ephesus, and Colossae to pray that he would be given boldness to preach the gospel, he expected them to pray for a Yes answer. That's what we usually mean when we exclaim, "God answered my prayer!" But how often are we able to say that? How many Yes answers do we get to our prayers?

Not enough! Not enough times when we find ourselves in that position of spiritual power where we *know* that the prayer is going to be answered. Not enough times when we see impossible obstacles come tumbling down before the invisible power of God. Not enough times when we present the need of some person before God with that sense of absolute confidence that the need will be met—and then it is! Not enough times when we find ourselves praying in such unity with other believers that we can virtually see the answer before it comes.

There is one secret—one basic truth—which more than any other will turn the No and Wait into Yes. If we are willing to learn and put into practice this truth, we will see a dramatic increase in the percentage of Yes answers which we get to our prayers.

It is not an easy way. God's ways seldom are. And yet, it is the nearest thing to a short-cut in the Christian life. Of course, there are no real short-cuts. But there *are* muddy detours which can be avoided. When you avoid an unnecessary detour, the effect on you is the same as if you'd discovered a short-cut; you bypass some of the stumbling and fumbling, the trial and error which eats up so much of our time and energy as Christians.

Consider these five keys to answered prayer:

1. Think God's Thoughts

Many of our prayers misfire right on the launching pad, because we begin with *our* thoughts rather than *God*'s thoughts. A situation comes up, and at once we lay hold on it with the grappling hooks of human reason.

When Jesus told His disciples that He must go to

Jerusalem, there to suffer and die, Peter rebuked Him and said, "God forbid, Lord! This shall never happen to you!" But Jesus answered, "Get behind me, Satan! You are a stumbling block to me, *because you think not as God, but as man.*" (Literal meaning of the Greek text, Matt. 16:23.) It is not enough to think about something that needs our prayer. We must think about it *the way God thinks about it.*

God's thoughts went beyond the suffering that Jesus would encounter in Jerusalem, beyond the rejection and humiliation, beyond the cross and the grave. God's thoughts looked forward to the Resurrection, to the triumphant Ascension, to the outpouring of the Holy Spirit, to Christ's glorious Second Coming, and His reign upon the earth.

Peter's response, typical of the response which is merely human, was *short-sighted.* He saw the immediate problem, but did not wait long enough to discover how that problem fitted into God's overall thinking. He jumped right in and surrounded the problem with an army of thoughts recruited in the backyard of his own human reason.

"My thoughts are not your thoughts, says the Lord . . . as the heavens are higher than the earth, so are my thoughts higher than your thoughts" (Isa. 55:8-9). In order to think God's thoughts, we must be prepared to go beyond the limits of mere human thinking. This does not mean that we become foolish or illogical. It just means that we submit our thinking to a higher wisdom than our own human reason. Instead of being bound by a short-sighted view which sees only the immediate situation, we begin to think about it the way God does.

This does not mean that we see and understand a situation fully, as God does. As a matter of fact, when we begin to think God's thoughts, we usually do not see His overall plan. We just have one thought that leads us along in a particular direction. The important thing is that it is *God*'s thought, and that we follow it. As we do, God will reveal more of His thoughts.

But how? That is the critical question. How can we think God's thoughts, so that we will experience more answers to our prayers? Of course we know that God has given us a norm for all revelation, the Scripture. But how does He apply Scripture to the specific circumstances of our daily lives? We know, for instance, that He wants the Church to "attain to the unity of the faith and of the knowledge of the Son of God, to mature manhood, to the measure of the stature of the fullness of Christ" (Eph. 4:13). But precisely how—in this church, at *this time*?

A Baptist minister in the South of England had the feeling that God wanted his congregation to set aside normal activities for a month, during which time the members should spend the time in prayer, seeking God's will for the congregation. He knew, however, that such a thought might be just his own human thinking, even though it seemed pious and spiritual. So he asked the Lord to *confirm* this thought if it really were from Him.

A short time later, one of his deacons came in to see him and said, "Pastor, the strangest thought has been coming to me. I can't shake it out of my mind, so I thought I ought to tell you. It's probably crazy, but this is it, that we should suspend all our activities here at church for a month or so, and just spend the time waiting on the Lord. Like I say, it's probably a crazy idea..."

When God's thoughts first come to us, they often appear impossible or unreasonable; like Peter, our natural tendency is to reject them. But if we wait and are alert, *God will confirm His thought to us*. One of the ways He does this is to bring the same thought to two or more people.

God's thoughts seldom concern just us, alone. He thinks about us in relation to others, especially fellow Christians. So if you believe that God may be beaming one of His thoughts to you, keep your eyes and ears open to see whether He is saying the same thing to others. It's one of the surest ways for Him to confirm His word to us. And it is a first giant step towards answered prayer. Jesus said, "If two of you agree on earth about anything they ask, it will be done for them by my Father in heaven" (Matt. 18:19). It isn't agreeing on *our* thoughts that brings answered prayer, but agreeing on *His* thoughts.

That is our first key to answered prayer: Think God's thoughts.

2. Feel God's Emotions

The musical play *1776* has a scene in which a communique from George Washington is read to the Continental Congress. He describes the desperate situation of the American cause, the discouragement among his troops, and concludes with the words, "Isn't anybody there? Doesn't anybody care?" The whole play resolves around the struggle of the men in the Continental Congress to rise above their petty personal feelings, to become united, heart and soul, in the cause of American independence. Any great cause must be bound together by a common emotion if it is to succeed.

Day after day the giant Goliath strutted up and down before the armies of Israel, taunting them, challenging them to battle. The men of Israel trembled. No one dared accept the giant's challenge.

When young David heard the giant's challenge, his heart was incensed within him. He felt the pain of the ridicule being heaped upon the armies of the Lord. He became indignant, and jealous for the Lord's honour.

"You come to me with a sword and with a spear and with a javelin," he called out to Goliath. "But I come to you in the name of the Lord of hosts, the God of the armies of Israel. This day the Lord will deliver you into my hand" (1 Sam. 17:45-46).

David's heart was filled with God's feelings. There was no room for the fear which had immobilized the men of Israel.

Our prayers lack power because too often they are bound up and immobilized by our own emotions. They do not reflect God's feelings.

Does it surprise us to think of God as having feelings? The Bible makes that abundantly clear. God is tender hearted and compassionate. God is sorrowful; He grieves over His people. God becomes angry; He hates sin and wickedness.

Moreover, people and angels share God's emotion. Jesus wept over Jerusalem. The angels rejoice when a sinner repents. When Nehemiah heard about the desolation of the holy city Jerusalem, he sat down and wept for days.

God does not take seriously those who do not share His feelings. "This people honours me with their lips, but their *heart* is far from me" (Matt. 15:8). If our prayers are to be answered, we must not only think with God; we must *feel* with Him.

We saw, in thinking God's thoughts, that it is important to check signals with other Christians; God often confirms something by bringing the same thought to more than one person. This is even more true in regard to God's feelings. We will never learn to feel God's emotion all by ourselves.

Emotion, by its very nature, tends to be a shared experience. If you feel an emotion, it's almost impossible to keep it to yourself. Even if you try, those who know you best pick it up. "Say, what's bothering you? You're not yourself today." Or, "You look like the cat that swallowed the canary. What's up?" When you feel something, you tend to communicate it to others.

On the other side, when others feel something, you pick it up from them. Have you ever picked up a mood from someone else? You may have started out the day happy and confident, but then you run into a long-faced pessimist, and the whole mood of your day takes on a sombre hue. Or, you may have been chugging along on two cylinders until a bright-eyed child bursts into the room, enthusiasm spilling out of every spigot, and all at once you find yourself perking up.

Emotion is contagious. That's why the writer to the Hebrews tells his people not to neglect to meet together where they can stir one another up to *love* and good works, where they can *encourage* one another (Heb. 10:24–25).

Where we stick to ourselves, or meet in non-Christian settings, the feelings that tend to get expressed are *our* feelings. Even when we meet together as Christians, too often we simply vent our own feelings. We need to be sensitive to what *God* feels, and express that. Because what we express will spread to others.

An Anglican church official said that the most promising hope for peace in Northern Ireland was the interdenominational charismatic prayer groups which brought Protestants and Catholics together. In one neighbourhood of Belfast, three Protestant girls came into a Catholic neighbourhood at night to attend one of these prayer groups.

"Don't you realize that you could be killed?" the Catholic people said.

"We have considered that carefully," the girls answered, "and we are prepared to lay down our lives for you."

They could have let their hearts fill up with the bitterness and mistrust that surrounded them. They could have given way to fear and uncertainty. But they let God put *His* emotion into their hearts—sorrow over His people, separated by hatred and bitterness; love for those who belonged to "them", but were His children nevertheless. And as they expressed this feeling, it spread. The Catholics opened their hearts to the same feeling; walls of prejudice began to crumble.

This is our second key: If we want our prayers to be answered, we must feel God's emotion.

3. *Desire God's Plan*

You can think God's thoughts, and feel God's emotions, yet still stand on the sidelines as an observer.

This is the step of personal commitment. This is where God's thoughts and God's feelings become your personal concern. You not only know what God knows and feel what He feels, but now *you want what God wants*.

"I would rather be a doorkeeper in the house of my God than dwell in the tents of wickedness" (Ps. 84 : 10). The psalmist would give up all earthly honours and accept the lowest position in God's house, so intense was his desire to be with God. Notice that the psalmist contrasted a life in the tents of wickedness with a life in the house of God. Desire for God's plan increases only as we let loose our desire for some other plan. In order to desire God's plan, we must be ready to sacrifice anything that stands in the way of that plan.

Many of our prayers go unanswered because we try to serve God and obey God without really desiring His plan. We feel a certain obligation to God, and so we give a little and do a little. But whether anything comes of it or not doesn't too deeply move us. Once we've done our duty, we can go back to the thing we really desire, which is our own plan, our own life lived the way we want to live it.

We need to become so deeply involved in the plans of God that if they fall, we go down with them. We need to become sensitive to the things God wants us to give up, in order that He can kindle within us a desire for His plan. "Thy kingdom come!" must become more than a phrase learned by repetition. It must become the consuming passion of our lives.

Loren Cunningham,* founder of "Youth With a

* The author is indebted to Mr. Cunningham for the format of this chapter.

Mission", tells how God showed him a new field of
ministry which was financially impossible to under-
take. But as he realized that this was God's thought,
not his, and as he began to feel God's emotion behind
it, he found it harder and harder to dismiss.

"Lord, what do you want us to do?" he asked.

"Give *everything*," God told him. "Go right down to
nothing."

When they gave everything they had and went
down to nothing, they began to desire this plan with
all their heart and soul. And that was when God began
to answer their prayers in miraculous ways. In order to
get answers to our prayers, we must desire God's plan.
And in order to desire God's plan, we must sacrifice
anything that stands in the way of that plan.

This is our third key to answered prayer: Desire
God's plan.

4. Speak God's Words

Thinking, feeling, desiring—we think of these as being
essentially *silent* expressions even though, as we have
seen, they involve real commitment. But there comes a
point in our prayers when we must *speak out*. We
must declare God's word for a particular situation. We
must put our faith on the line.

God thought about a world; He desired a world. But
the world came into existence only when God *spoke*.

Jesus thought about raising Lazarus even before He
arrived at Bethany, where Lazarus had died. He experienced God's emotion at the graveside, and wept,
for He said, "I can do nothing of my own accord, but
only what I see the Father doing" (John 5:19). He

knew that it was God's plan for Lazarus to be raised, and He desired that plan. But Lazarus remained in the tomb until Jesus cried out, "Lazarus, come forth!" The spoken word energizes God's plans.

Why do so many of our spoken prayers go unanswered? Why do our petitions pour out in a torrent, while our answers come back in a trickle? It is because we speak *our* words instead of *God*'s words.

Our words may express only a wish or a hope. God's words express a divine intention which God will back up. "As the rain and the snow come down from heaven, and return not thither but water the earth ... giving seed to the sower and bread to the eater, so shall my word be that goes forth from my mouth; it shall not return to me empty, but it shall accomplish that which I purpose" (Isa. 55:10–11). If we want our prayers to be answered, we must come to the place where we speak not our words, but God's words— where the words of our prayers on earth are an echo of the words which God has already spoken in heaven. Jesus said, "I do nothing on my own authority but speak thus as the Father taught me" (John 8:28). That was why His prayers were so effective. He spoke God's words.

Speaking God's words, of course, is closely related to thinking God's thoughts, but it is not the same. Thinking God's thoughts can go on quietly inside us. Our desire for God's plan can be pretty much a private commitment. But when we speak God's words, the commitment becomes public. And this poses two opposite and equal dangers.

On the one hand, we are in danger of speaking out merely our own desire or ambition. On the other hand, for fear that we will not be speaking God's word, we clam up and say nothing. What is the answer to this dilemma?

St. Paul said, "Let two or three prophets speak, and let the others weigh what is said" (1 Cor. 14:29). The prophet might be speaking God's word, according to the best of his understanding. But it's possible that he didn't get the whole message, or didn't understand it fully. So his words are weighed by the others. If we want to learn to speak God's words, we must be willing to submit our prayers and utterances to evaluation and correction by fellow Christians.

This will mean some radical re-evaluation of our whole attitude towards prayer. If a person makes a false or ill-founded statement in a discussion, it is called to his attention. But if someone does the same kind of thing in prayer, it is swallowed up in pious silence. Speaking God's words is no easy thing. Where did we ever get the idea that we could learn to do it with never a bit of help, never any correction or guidance? If we want to speak God's word, we must be ready to enter into the "School of Prayer" in the literal sense of that term. Through help and correction from fellow Christians, we can learn to distinguish God's word. Then our speaking will not be just words in the air, but the release of power.

This is our fourth key to answered prayer: Speak God's word.

5. Do God's Works

If we have started out thinking God's thoughts, and followed through to speaking His words, the chances are that we've got ourselves into an *impossible situation*! And right here is where a lot of prayer answers get lost. We see the impossible situation, and we push the panic button. "Must have made a mistake somewhere! This is *impossible*!" The tragedy is, at this point the prayer is as good as answered. All it needs now is that *we do what is possible*—and trust God for what is impossible.

The "possible" may be some kind of a commitment or sacrifice on our part—not enough to do the whole job, but the full extent of what we are able to do. It's the story of the little boy with his five loaves and two fish. All that was possible for him was to give them to Jesus. But it was all God needed to release the miracle. "Doing God's works" means to do everything that is possible and trust God for the rest.

This is our fifth key to answered prayer: Do God's works.

> Think God's Thoughts ...
> Feel God's Emotion ...
> Desire God's Plan ...
> Speak God's Word ...
> Do God's Works ...

What does it all add up to? Jesus put it this way: "The Son can do nothing of his own accord, but only what he sees the Father doing; for whatever he does, that the Son does likewise" (John 5:19). *The secret of answered prayer is to find out what God is doing—and do the same thing.*

CHAPTER TWELVE

Praying in the Name of Jesus

One of the most important phrases in the life of prayer is "*in the Name of Jesus*". Attached to those five little words is one of the most remarkable promises of Scripture, the promise of *unlimited answer to prayer*.

Now the problem is this: Many of us have prayed, using this phrase, and yet our prayers have gone unanswered. Why?

The reason is that we have had an inadequate understanding, not only of what this phrase means, but of what it involves. Even more pointedly, *what it involves us in*.

The first thing we need is a framework for understanding the significance of this phrase. Consider this illustration:

One summer, during my college days, I travelled as a field representative for a well-known seed company. Before they sent us out to our territories, they put us through a two-week crash training programme.

In one of the morning sessions, the teacher threw out the remark, "Remember, you're selling seeds, not chewing gum and candy."

We glanced at one another, puzzled. Of course we were selling seeds. We knew that. That's what we were hired for. What in the world did he mean?

He went on to explain that sometimes salesmen had tried to augment their income by carrying another little line along with them. After them they had talked to a merchant about his seed order, they would bring out the chewing gum and candy. The chewing gum and candy, of course, were free-loading on the seed company, which was covering all the travel expenses and providing the dealer contacts.

"But even more important than that," the man told us, "we don't want to tie our reputation to anything except our own product. If you go in as a representative of our company and sell a man something we have nothing to do with, in that man's mind you've tied us to that other product. Our seeds we are able and willing to back up, not chewing gum and candy."

Not one of us took issue with what this man said to us. It made perfectly good sense. The company that employs you has the right to your undivided loyalty and service when you are on the job. Anyone who enters the employ of someone else sets aside his private activities when he's on the job. St. Paul said, "A soldier does not get entangled in civilian pursuits." The activities and objectives of the employer now become his personal concern. What he does, he does as a representative of his employer. He does not act simply in his own name, but in the name of his employer.

This is the kind of framework we need in order to understand what it means to pray, "in the Name of Jesus". When we pray, we are representing Him and His interests. He has a great plan for the redemption of mankind. He wants us to present the plan to the Father in prayer, in order to obtain from the Father the resources and support needed to carry out the plan.

Jesus uses us to carry out this prayer operation in a particular territory. To pray "in the Name of Jesus", therefore, means that Jesus employs us to help carry out His work of prayer.

Now in order to represent someone else, we have to know what that person is like, what his plans are, and what he expects of us. We have to move from thinking and reacting according to our own point of view and begin thinking and reacting according to his point of view. If we are to enter into the promises of Scripture concerning praying "in the Name of Jesus", we must begin to look at the whole business of prayer from Jesus' point of view.

Get To Know His Purpose

In John 16:23, Jesus says, "In that day you will ask nothing of me." By "that day" Jesus means the day when He would come back to His disciples after the Resurrection. It refers to the relationship between disciples and the risen Lord. What Jesus says here, then, can be applied to Christians today as well, who through faith have a relationship with the risen Lord.

When Jesus says that we will ask nothing of Him, He does not mean that we can never pray to Him. In John 14:14, He says plainly, "If you ask anything in my name, I will do it." A Christian may certainly pray to Jesus.

But Jesus is telling us here that our praying is going to pass through a basic change in its point of view, which is the same as saying that up until now you have prayed in your own name. You have asked for things that *you* wanted, prayed about things that *you* had a concern for, presented petitions to God in *your own name*.

But now, when I come back to you, you will begin to pray in *My* name. Your first thought will not be, "Lord, help me! Lord, please do this, or bless that." Rather, you will pause and ask, "Lord, what is *Your* purpose here? What prayers do *You* want me to pray?"

Instead of presenting your petitions to Jesus, you will begin to inquire about His purpose. That's what it means to pray in Jesus' Name. You are preparing to be His representative, and in order to be that, you have to know what His purpose or goal is so you can make it your own.

Do you see what a radical change this will be for many people? To set aside *our* purposes and inquire first about *Jesus'* purposes. It's like the two-year-old son of a friend of ours. One afternoon we went over to their house for a visit. On the coffee table were some soft-centre candies that the little boy liked very much. The mother told him to take one over and give it to me. He picked one up in his fingers and started towards me, holding the candy in front of him. As he looked at the candy, it seemed to be drawn like a magnet towards his mouth, and before he got across to me, he had eaten the candy himself. Candy was something for *him* to eat. He wasn't yet ready to adopt the idea that it was for others too.

Unfortunately, even Christian books on prayer keep alive the idea that prayer is primarily a means of meeting *our* needs. Prayer, especially prayer *in the Name of Jesus*, is primarily a means of fulfilling *Jesus'* purposes.

That's why the Lord's Prayer begins with petitions for *God*'s Name to be hallowed, for *His* kingdom to come, for *His* will to be done.

George McCausland says that he experienced a breakthrough in intercessory prayer when he began to pray with a view to God's purpose in the matter. He had been in the habit of praying in this vein: "Lord, please help this person (for whom I have a concern). Lord, please see to this need (that I feel), Lord, come here; Lord, go there." He changed his approach, and began to pray something like this: "Lord, what can I do to help You with Your plan—for this person, for this need or situation?" The change was almost immediate. He was praying with new authority and power. He was no longer representing his own interests to God—he was presenting Jesus' interests to God. He was Jesus' personal representative, and therefore Jesus' purposes were his purposes. If we want to pray "in the Name of Jesus", we have to get to know what Jesus' purposes are, so we can present them to God.

Get To Know His Product

No salesman will mark up any records on the sales chart who doesn't know his product, and know it thoroughly. If Jesus is employing us in this prayer business, then we need to know what prayer can do, what kind of capability it has.

Remember who the "customer" is—*God*! You come to Him with a prayer (it's Jesus' prayer—you're just representing His interests in this particular territory). You have to "sell" God on the value of this prayer, so He will release whatever it is that the prayer calls for, just as a customer releases a certain amount of money when the salesman presents a product which he sees he can use.

In the Bible Jesus presents God to us as One who *wants to be convinced*. In two parables in the Gospel of Luke, Jesus tells us to persist in prayer until we overcome God's sales resistance (Luke 11:5–8; 18:1–8).

Martin Luther once prayed for his friend Philip Melanchthon, who was sick. He said, "I backed God into a corner. I reminded Him of all His promises concerning prayer. And I told Him that I just could not continue to believe in Him if He didn't heal Philip!"

Now that is what we might call a "hard sell". Not recommended for the beginner! But it makes a point. Luther knew that he had a good product. He knew that God not only liked prayer, He needed prayer. He has chosen to run His whole kingdom by prayer.

The prayers of Jesus are as necessary to the running of God's kingdom as flight fuel is necessary for a jet-liner. When a fuel salesman from Shell Oil Company calls on the purchasing agent of an airline, he knows that he has a product that the airline can't get along without. And we have a big advantage over the salesman from Shell. He has to compete with salesmen from half a dozen other companies. There's no competition with God: He has a built-in favouritism for the prayers of Jesus. He knows that they are the only prayers that have power and authority to build His kingdom.

What would you think of someone who came and offered you a £100 piece of merchandise for £37.50? You'd wonder if it was defective, or a cheap imitation. Jesus expects us to get full value for His prayers. When we pray in Jesus' Name, we dare expect great things from God because the prayers of Jesus command premium return. Jesus said, "I expect you to go right on doing the works that I do, getting the same kind of answers to prayer that I get."

If we are *not* getting answers to prayer, perhaps we need to take a closer look at the *product* we've been peddling. Is it *His* product? Or have we been dabbling in chewing gum and candy?

In practical terms this means that before we present a petition to God, we have to do some careful *asking*, and *listening*. "Lord Jesus, what do *you* want here? What is *Your* prayer for this person?'" As we get quiet inside, and listen, He will tell us the kind of prayer which He wants us to offer the Father on this occasion.

When the Father sees that prayer, and notes the trademark of His own Son on it, you'll be surprised at how eager He is to close the deal.

Get To Know His Plan for You

Jesus has a personal plan for each one of us whom He employs in this business of prayer. When we were taking the training course at the seed company, one of their top salesmen came in and gave us some instruc-tion one afternoon.

"He handles the Woolworth account," we were told. "We don't want any of you eager beavers going in and calling on any Woolworth stores. That's handled at the national level."

To pray in Jesus' Name means to work in the territory He assigns to us. Agnes Sanford calls it "my bundle". Jesus puts prayers in our bundle which are appropriate to our spiritual age and experience. It's consistent with His personality, which is a nurturing, encouraging personality.

As we focus upon His purpose, and as we get to know His 'product' (i.e., come to see the power of prayer), we will also begin to feel His personal interest in us *and in our prayer progress*—just as a good employer is interested in seeing his salesmen catch hold and begin to bring in results.

I once had the privilege of visiting Sarah Covington. She is a member of the congregation which grew out of the Azusa Street Mission, which was the centre of the great Pentecostal revival in 1906. She is the only member of that congregation still alive who lived in the time of the revival.

As we talked, she kept referring to "something new I'm asking the Lord about". She wouldn't tell us what it was. But we got the feeling that it was a pretty definite business between her and the Lord. It was like she had been given a new territory, and she was just getting acquainted with it. She was past 90, but there was no diminishing of her enthusiasm. While we were there, she got two or three phone calls, and it was always something to do with the Lord and His business.

In this business, there's no unemployment, no retirement. When Jesus takes you on, it's for life. In fact, for eternity.